LEADERSHIP REDEFINED
THE 12 X'S OF SUCCESS
FOR TODAY'S LEADER

dave weber

ISBN-13: 978-0-9760628-5-1

LCCN: 2012909281

Cover design and photos by Kevin Heffner.

ACKNOWLEDGEMENTS

When I started to think about writing this book, I felt a bit insecure about the project, despite the fact that I had the support of family and colleagues, and I'd already had a book under my belt. *Sticks & Stones Exposed: The Power of Our Words,* continues to surpass industry expectations, and I am still frequently asked to present on the topic across the country.

But this was different. I didn't feel like I had anything to say about leadership that other people would want to read. I mean really...*who am I to be an authority on such a topic*? I've never run a Fortune 500 company (or a Fortune 5000 company for that matter). I've never been brought into a failing organization and led a dramatic turnaround. I've never even coached a professional sports team...you know, things that might inspire others to read about my wisdom and experience.

I'm a husband, father, owner of a small business, Sunday School teacher, mediocre golfer, and dog owner. What do I have to say about leadership?

Well, as you will see, plenty. Once I began to listen to my bride Tina, my kids, Lindsey and Logan, and my amazing colleagues at Weber Associates, Inc.: Kevin Heffner, Jill Phillips, Becky Spain, and Ynes "Rosa" Rosas, I realized that there were a number of very specific disciplines that had become a part of my "leadership practices."

Thanks to all of you for encouraging me to get out of my comfort zone and bring this book to life. Your constant encouragement was a great source of inspiration. Thank you, Dad, for introducing me to the 12 X's and for implementing them in your own life so that I could see they really work.

Blane Bachelor, you are a gifted writer and I so enjoy partnering with you. Thanks for your wit, your insights, and your dedication.

And finally, I would like to give a special thanks to John C. Maxwell, whose work helped inspire this book. Your ideas, especially your gracious modeling of the 12th X, "Extend a Helping Hand," are truly the reason this book is a reality.

DEDICATION

This book is dedicated to those who lead.
Whether the setting is a classroom, a boardroom, a dugout, or
a kitchen, whether you have the "title" of leader or not.
Lead well.

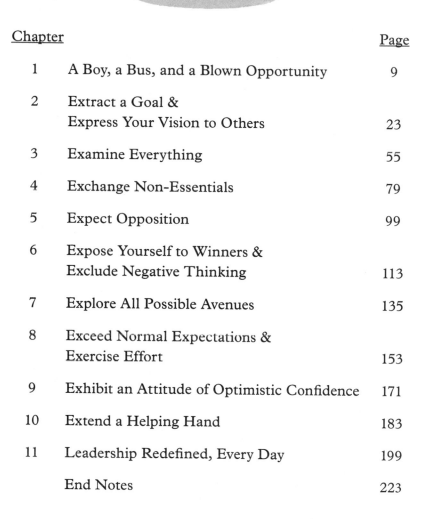

TABLE OF CONTENTS

Chapter

Page

1   A Boy, a Bus, and a Blown Opportunity   9

2   Extract a Goal &
     Express Your Vision to Others   23

3   Examine Everything   55

4   Exchange Non-Essentials   79

5   Expect Opposition   99

6   Expose Yourself to Winners &
     Exclude Negative Thinking   113

7   Explore All Possible Avenues   135

8   Exceed Normal Expectations &
     Exercise Effort   153

9   Exhibit an Attitude of Optimistic Confidence   171

10   Extend a Helping Hand   183

11   Leadership Redefined, Every Day   199

     End Notes   223

CHAPTER 1
A BOY, A BUS, AND
A BLOWN OPPORTUNITY

The key to successful leadership today
is influence, not authority.
- Ken Blanchard

It was a wet, dreary October morning as a single mom and her six-year-old son prepared for their day. It was still dark outside as they ate their cereal.

The mother glanced down at her watch and realized time was getting away from them. "Let's hurry up, buddy," she said, noticing that he was moving a little slowly that morning. "I don't want you to miss the bus. Run upstairs, brush your teeth, and get your backpack. I'll drive you to the bus stop so you won't get wet."

At the bus stop, they waited for the bus, which was running a few minutes late, as it usually did on rainy days. "Good-bye, Mommy. I love you!" said the boy, as he scurried out of the car.

"Bye, buddy. Have a great day!" his mom replied, watching as he struggled up those three almost-too-big steps and took his usual seat halfway to the back. As the bus pulled away, she saw his face in the window as he waved excitedly. She returned the wave with an equal amount of energy, smiling at her son as the bus pulled out of view. Then she headed back home to get ready for work.

Meanwhile, the bus proceeded through the neighborhood, collecting children at stops along the way. After about a dozen stops, the little boy left his seat and approached the bus driver.

"Excuse me," he said, almost crying. "I just got sick in my seat."

Great, the bus driver thought. *This kid has just puked in my bus. Just what I need on an already lousy day.* He barked: "Then you need to go home!" and opened the door to the bus, motioning the little boy off.

With the wide eyes of the other children heavy upon him, the little boy, sniffling and embarrassed, slowly climbed back down those three steep steps. The door closed behind him, and the bus pulled away, leaving him standing on the side of the street in the rain.

The door closed behind him, and the bus pulled away, leaving him standing on the side of the street in the rain.

Nearby, another mom had just watched her daughter get on that same bus. She was standing on the front stoop of her house under an umbrella. She saw the bus approach the stop, the door open, and her daughter climb aboard. Then she waited for the bus to pull away.

But it didn't. After a few minutes, the door opened again, and she watched a little boy step off, the door close, and the bus pull away.

What in the world? she thought.

She then turned her attention to the little boy as he, too, watched the bus roll away. He looked up the street in one direction and then down the other. Then his chin dropped to his chest, and he began to cry. It was obvious he had no clue where he was, where to go, or what to do.

With one last glance around, the little boy started walking in the opposite direction the bus had gone.

Every sense of intuition – a parent's, a woman's, a concerned neighbor's – was sounding an alarm in that mother, and she took off after the little boy. She heard his sobs before she could see his face, and as soon as she caught up to him she softly called out, "Hey there, are you ok?"

The little boy turned around, his tears mingling with the rain on his face. "I'm sick, and the bus driver told me I have to go home, but I don't know where I am!" he wept.

The mother's heart broke for this little boy, seeing how distraught he was about being dropped off the bus, feeling sick with nobody there to help him, on a strange street as the rain came down. She imagined her young daughter in the same position, and although she had a very busy day ahead of her, getting this child home safe and sound became her number one priority.

In about 20 minutes, she succeeded. After some trial and error exploring the neighborhood, they finally found the little boy's house, where his mother was pulling out of the driveway on her way to work.

Upon seeing her son walk up with a strange woman, the little boy's mother quickly jumped out of her car and demanded to know what was going on. The woman immediately introduced herself and described what she had seen transpire at the bus stop in front of her home.

You can only imagine how grateful the little boy's mom was and, after exchanging phone numbers, she hugged the woman tightly. And sure enough, as she embraced her son, she could feel that he was running a fever. Once inside, she got him back into his pajamas, gave him some Tylenol and tucked him into bed.

Then she turned her attention to the phone in the kitchen, and the people on the receiving end of her calls.

A Very Mad Mom

Before I tell you what happened next, put yourself in the shoes of Mom. How are you feeling right now? What is running through your mind? Disbelief? Anger? Confusion? Frustration? Disappointment?

All of the above?

You bet.

Mom, experiencing a sickening mix of all of those horrible emotions, dialed the number of her son's school and described what had just happened to him that morning.

The woman who answered the phone at the school replied, "Sorry, ma'am, that's not my job. I can't help you with that. Call transportation!" and hung up.

So *now* how are you feeling, Mom?

How about *stratospheric* levels of disbelief, rage, confusion, frustration, and disappointment? Honestly, I think I'd be ready to rip the lips off somebody!

After she hung up the phone, the mom did not call transportation. She didn't call the superintendent's office. She didn't call the school board office, a friend, or her attorney. She called a nationally syndicated radio talk show and was immediately put on the air to tell her story, and you can bet she vented every ounce of her charged emotions about what had happened to her young son to thousands of shocked listeners.

For the next several hours, it became "Bash Public Schools" day on the radio as people all across the country called in with their horror stories. Every employee of public schools got a black eye that day, as listeners vented to a nationwide audience their own frustrations in dealing with school system employees.

Every employee of public schools got a black eye that day. Why did this happen?

Why did this happen? Because two people who had the opportunity to positively influence the situation chose, for whatever reason, not to.

The Unaware Leader

If this incident sounds familiar to any of you reading this, especially those who live in Georgia, it should. It actually happened in a school district in northwest Georgia, which I shall not name.

What's seriously unfortunate about this incident, besides the angst of the little boy and his mother, is that it never needed to happen. Had the bus driver and/or the school employee who answered the phone responded differently, they could have probably received a pat on the back from their supervisors, a word or note of appreciation from a concerned mother, and the possibility of establishing their school in a positive light in the eyes of the community. Instead, they ended up unemployed the next day.

They didn't understand they were leaders.

Maybe they were simply incompetent employees. Maybe they were both having rough days and making uncharacteristically bad decisions.

But it's likely they didn't understand that they were leaders.

Leaders?, you could be wondering. *Seriously? A bus driver? An administrative assistant in an elementary school? No way, Dave!*

Well, *yes way,* I say. Let's take a closer look at what being a leader can mean.

Leadership Redefined

Think, for a minute, about a chessboard. What piece first comes to your mind? The king, probably, or the queen, or maybe a knight. No surprise: These are the most visible, the most powerful pieces. They have the most prestige. We like how the knight can jump over other pieces, how the rooks and bishops can fly all the way across the board in certain directions. And we do everything we can to protect the all-important king, while respecting the power of the queen.

But the lowly pawns, like the one on the cover of this book, who thinks about them? Aren't they the throwaway pieces, the ones that can be sacrificed on the way to victory? Not to a chess master. One savvy move with a pawn or two can mean the difference between victory and defeat. The influence a pawn can have on a game of chess is extremely powerful, as is the influence that we as everyday individuals – even if we might consider ourselves just lowly pawns – can have on this game called life.

The influence a pawn can have on a game of chess is extremely powerful, as is the influence that we as individuals can have on this game called life.

This is what Leadership Redefined is all about. It's not about title, authority, or superiority. It is about using your influence *right where you are* to positively impact what is going on around you. It's about picking up the ball and running with it. It's about doing the best you can with what you have, and not settling for anything less.

A Traditional Take On Leadership

Some people define leadership by a title. Others define a leader by the amount of responsibility or authority one has, or by how many people a person oversees, or how much money one may have. Sometimes, a leader has a combination of all of those. And there are dozens of books on the market, as well as life coaches, management gurus, and financial whizzes, whose sole focus is teaching people how to achieve or attain this kind of larger-scale leadership – and the wealth and prestige that it often leads to.

This book does not fall into that category.

I wrote this book to reframe the idea of what it means to be a leader, to help people understand that the idea of leadership isn't just some lofty goal or state of being reserved for presidents, CEOs, and the rich. In doing so, I hope to help you better understand the characteristics and strengths present in all good leaders, which I also happen to believe are present in each and every one of us. See, leadership takes many shapes and forms, and no matter who you are, or what you do, or how much wealth or material possessions you have (or don't), you have the ability to become a leader in your own life – and profoundly change it, and the lives of those around you, for the better.

It's not about title, authority, or superiority. It is about using your influence right where you are to positively impact what is going on around you.

Before we go any further, let's address a few of the questions I'm sure are bouncing around in some of your heads. *Wait a second, Dave, I'm not so sure I want to be a leader, anyway,* some of you might be thinking. *I'm pretty happy as a follower, part of the group. I take direction well and I prefer someone else to be in the driver's seat, I'm not very good at making decisions, and I don't like stress and...*

And if I listen closely enough, I can hear others saying, *What about that saying that goes, Too many chefs spoil the soup? Or that if you have too many chiefs, you can't have a tribe? Isn't there such a thing as too many leaders?*

Whoa. You're falling into the traditional paradigm of what leadership is. This book is all about changing that, starting with your own sphere of influence. You see, being a leader doesn't have to mean you must have an A-type personality or your sights set on becoming CEO of your company or superintendent of the school district. It doesn't mean you have to become the president of your son's Little League. It doesn't mean you have to oversee a department of dozens of direct reports. It doesn't mean you have millions of dollars or Facebook fans or followers on Twitter.

At the heart of this book is this goal: Helping you discover, understand, and internalize a new concept of leadership.

While standards like responsibility, authority, financial standing, or occupation can be universal measures to establish leaders, being a leader can have a much more subtle, but no less powerful, definition. For the purposes of this book, we'll look at leadership like this:

A leader is anyone who has influence.

The key word in that sentence is *influence* – not power, not wealth, not status, not looks. Influence can equal leadership, for good or for bad. Of course, good leadership is what we're striving for, and it boils down to positively influencing the situation. That's what the rest of this book will focus on: understanding and honing our ability to lead well, to become good leaders, by positively influencing the situation.

Now, with a definition like that, who can be a leader? Anyone – even if they don't have a title, occupation, or demeanor that would necessarily imply it. Take a look at any group of kindergartners on the playground. Not one of those little stinkers has a title, but there is definitely someone in charge, influencing what's going on. While CEOs are certainly considered leaders, receptionists can be, too. Principals are definite leaders, but custodians can just as easily demonstrate leadership qualities in their jobs. While most people traditionally look to the top of an organization or department for leadership *(in theory, that is!)*, the highest performing groups in companies, schools, clubs, or sports teams have members who demonstrate leadership at every level. These "leaders without the title" have latched on to the profound reality that because they have influence, they lead.

These "leaders without a title" have latched on to the profound reality that because they have influence, they lead.

Here's another way to look at it: While leaders can certainly have a traditional sense of power and responsibility – like the king and queen pieces on a chessboard, for example – the pawn can also act as a leader, too. That's because, just like all the other pieces, the pawn has the ability to influence the outcome of the game.

As we'll discuss, the road to becoming a leader starts not by looking at who, or what, you'll be leading. Instead, it starts by taking a good, hard look in the mirror – and then into the crystal ball of your life. You might be surprised at how big an impact seemingly small actions can have, both on the people and situations around you, as well as on your life itself.

Back To The Bus Debacle

Consider again the school bus driver and the administrative assistant who answered the phone that rainy morning. Did either of them have any sort of a title or job description that implied leadership in the traditional definition of leadership?

With a definition like that, who can be a leader? Anyone!

No. But they certainly had the power to influence the situation. They had the ability to lead another person – in their case, a distraught mother of one of the students within their own educational organization – to a positive, or at least a much less negative, outcome from the gaffe that happened to her son. Sadly, though, neither chose to influence the situation positively, a decision that in the end cost them their jobs.

But consider what could have happened had they recognized and acted on their respective influence as leaders in these redefined terms. Let's start with the bus driver. Generally speaking, bus drivers don't get their due respect when it comes to the enormous responsibility they take on – the lives of dozens of students are, literally, in their hands every day. While getting children to school safely day in and day out is an enormous task (and one that I believe deserves more recognition), in the particular case of the bus driver who booted the little boy off his bus, perhaps he viewed that responsibility too narrowly.

A broader, and more relevant, way to look at his task and the potential for his positive leadership and influence is this: The bus experience is often the very first contact that a student has with respect to his or her education every single day. The bus driver's face is the first face a student sees with respect to school. Consequently, any experience a student has on the bus or with the bus driver, good or bad, can make an indelible mark on the perception a child has of education, for better or worse.

In other words, while the bus driver certainly has to focus on the physical action of driving the bus, he or she also must focus on the emotional aspect of the students in his or her care. What do you think was the reaction of the little boy the next time he had to ride the bus to school? Do you think he thought about the ride, or the bus driver, or even school as a whole, in a positive light? Probably not. And this is something that possibly never occurred to the bus driver from northwest Georgia.

Now, consider the administrative assistant who took the mother's call before quickly referring her to another department and hanging up on her. Like the bus driver, she clearly didn't see herself in a leadership role, or else she would have stepped up to put this upset parent in touch with someone who could help set the predicament on a more positive course than it was headed. Of course, considering what had just happened to her son, the mother had plenty of reason to be furious already. But where the administrative assistant failed was in contributing to the mother's anger and frustration, instead of helping to offset it by making sure her call was routed to the correct department. Or giving the mother a name of someone she could speak with. Or taking her number, figuring out a correct department and contact name, and calling her back to relay this information, instead of making her navigate the infuriating phone system maze herself. Another opportunity for positive influence lost.

The bus driver and administrative assistant also missed another critical component: Becoming a leader – positively influencing a situation – doesn't have to require that much more time or effort than that with which you're already living your life. What it does require, however, is living it with a bit more *intention*.

Negative Intention

Which brings me to my next point: History – and daily life, for that matter – is full of examples of people who have great leadership skills but aren't great leaders, in the sense that they are not using their influence in a positive way. A few prominent ones come to mind: Adolf Hitler, Charles Manson, and Osama Bin Laden. These men were able to recruit thousands of followers to their causes and influence the outcome of the situation, but the horrors they inflicted on humanity were appalling and heartbreaking. They didn't use their influence for good – only for personal gain, at the expense of staggering amounts of pain, loss, and suffering.

Obviously, these examples represent the worst of the worst. But take a look at your own life: Can you think of someone who has great leadership potential but instead of being a positive influence, they are toxic to the team, work group, or organization?

Can you think of someone who has great leadership potential but instead of being a positive influence, they are toxic to the team?

Even more commonplace, consider bullies at schools. These despicable characters usually manage to recruit a crony or two to pick on other kids; in other words, they clearly have influence and the natural ability to lead others. But that doesn't make them good leaders. Instead, they're using their influence to harm and hurt.

It's interesting to note that these kinds of negative leaders might share some common character traits with the kind of leaders we want to emulate – confidence, for example, and the ability to think outside the box. And although we'll be looking closer at some of those common traits, this is obviously not the type of leadership I'm striving to develop in this book.

By the same token, there are some universal characteristics great leaders display, and strategies they utilize, that we can all learn and benefit from, and use to positively influence the world around us. I call them the 12 Xs of Success, and they form the basis of this book. They are:

- Extract a Dream
- Express Your Vision to Others
- Exercise Effort
- Examine Everything
- Exchange Non-Essentials
- Expect Opposition
- Exclude Negative Thinking
- Expose Yourself to Winners
- Explore All Possible Avenues
- Exceed Normal Expectations
- Exhibit an Attitude of Optimistic Confidence
- Extend a Helping Hand

You'll discover how, without much effort, the simple focus of becoming more intentional with affecting a positive outcome will lead to some pretty cool things happening in your life. People will be more drawn toward you. Your relationships, both personal and professional, will start to perk up. Your boss, coworkers, students, and peers will view you with a new sense of respect, admiration, and appreciation. And, if you have your eye on bigger things – like getting a raise or promotion, or you're ready for more responsibility at work – what you'll learn here will enable you to achieve those goals, too.

At its core, Leadership Redefined is all about being intentional in leading or influencing the world around us to make our lives and those of people around us better, more enjoyable, and more fulfilling. And what's not to like about that?

So let's start leading.

EXPLORE ON YOUR OWN

1. Whom do you believe you have influence over? Or, who can/do you influence? How?

2. Think of someone whom you wouldn't view as a typical leader. Can you think of a time when this person surprised you by taking charge of a situation, influencing its outcome, or acting in a leadership role? Describe the circumstances.

3. Name a time when, although you were not the leader, you intentionally chose to positively influence a situation. Describe the scene and what happened.

4. What examples can you think of when you were on the receiving end of someone who didn't take advantage of his or her opportunity to act in a leadership role? What can you learn from those experiences to apply to your own life?

5. How could you be viewing your responsibility in certain settings too narrowly?

6. In the opening story, how did the second mother demonstrate leadership?

7. How can you lead by serving others?

8. How could you live your personal life with a bit more intention?

9. How could you view and do your job with more intention?

10. Armed with the concept of Leadership Redefined, what areas of your life do you hope to most apply these principles?

CHAPTER 2

EXTRACT A GOAL & EXPRESS YOUR VISION TO OTHERS

A leader is a dealer in hope.
- Napoleon Bonaparte

Pop quiz: What do the following quotes, excerpts, scenarios, people, and finally, poem have in common?

a.) Proverbs 29:18, which states: "Where there is no vision the people perish."

b.) While the ancient Greeks were the big men on Planet Earth, Plato, the great philosopher, said, "The ship that has not set its course finds no wind favorable."

c.) In his classic *Alice's Adventures in Wonderland,* author Lewis Carroll conveys Alice's confusion about her next steps in some beautifully crafted dialogue with the Cheshire Cat. "Which way should I go?" she asks. The ever-wily cat replies: "That depends on where you want to go." Alice then says: "Oh, I don't much care where," to which the cat replies, "Then it doesn't matter which way you go." (Pretty insightful creature, that cat.)

d.) Self-help sections in bookstores

e.) Maya Angelou, Sir Winston Churchill, President Barack Obama, and Billy Graham f.) A poem I learned from my father decades ago but, alas, have no attribution for:

> *There once was a teacher*
> *Whose principle feature*
> *Was hidden in quite an odd way.*
> *Students by millions,*
> *Possibly zillions,*
> *Followed him all of the day.*
> *When finally seen*
> *By the scholarly dean*
> *And asked how he managed the deed,*
> *He raised three fingers*
> *And said, "All you swingers*
> *Need only to follow my lead.*
> *To rise from a zero*
> *To big campus hero*
> *To answer these questions you'll strive:*
> *Where am I going?*
> *How will I get there?*
> *And how will I know I've arrived?"*

The common thread between all these examples is that, in one way or another, they illustrate the power of having a goal, target, or objective in our lives. On another level, they relate to a basic yearning of the human psyche: to fulfill our dreams.

And dreams and goals can be powerful motivators behind behavior. They can be the drivers that move us to stay later, push harder, work faster. They give our lives meaning, value, desire, and hope. In addition to enabling us to see a better future for ourselves, having hope – and, just as importantly, the ability to inspire hope in others – is an underlying trait present in all leaders.

You see, hope in the future brings power to the present. This is a concept that the best leaders understand and internalize. Consider British Prime Minister Sir Winston Churchill, for example. The man's name alone is synonymous with inspiration, and his superb leadership stemmed from his ability to stir hope in 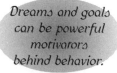 others when there seemed to be none. Even in the darkest days of the Battle of Britain, his words inspired and lifted a country exhausted and battered by war onto victory. Today, Churchill's legacy of leadership is still associated with his with remarkable perseverance. His "never give in" speech (although it's often misquoted as "never give up") is often brought up when falling down seems far easier than forging ahead.

Dreams and goals can be powerful motivators behind behavior.

In modern-day politics, President Barack Obama's ascent to the most powerful position in the world was based on his ability to bring hope to a public weary of two wars, a stagnant economy, and increasing partisanship in government. Regardless of where you fall on the political spectrum, it's hard to argue that Obama's unyielding message of hope helped get him elected in 2008. His campaign slogans – "Hope and Change" and "Yes We Can" – took hold and became a rallying cry for many in the general population. Eventually, this little-known senator from Illinois (whose middle name is "Hussein" and whose surname rhymes with "Osama," I might add), became a household name. Obama was named the country's first African American president in November 2008.

Renowned poet and author Maya Angelou is another well-recognized figure whose life was enhanced by hope. Raised by her grandmother in the 1930s, Angelou lived a childhood fraught with struggles. She was raped when she was eight years old and then had a child at 17. She had every reason to be bitter, resentful, and angry at a world that had dealt her an awful hand.

But she didn't. She had hope.

So where did Angelou's hope come from? It came from a goal, a vision, a dream implanted in her young mind by her grandmother. Her grandmother would buy books by Horatio Alger, a 19th century writer who chronicled the rise of poor white boys who triumphed over all odds to become the leaders of burgeoning industries around the turn of the century.

Hope in the future brings power to the present.

In an interview in *World Traveler* magazine, Angelou credits her grandmother for guiding her through those dark days growing up. She would often tell Angelou: "If you walk up a path that somebody else told you to walk, and you look ahead and you don't like where you're going, and you look back and you don't want to return, step off the path. Pick yourself a brand new road."[1]

That guidance from her grandmother helped Angelou pick her own brand new road – in other words, her dream – from roots of poverty, violence, and suffering that most of us cannot even imagine. Angelou, now in her 70s, boasts a life full of awards and accomplishments: Pulitzer Prize-nominated author, three Presidential appointments, fluency in six languages, Tony-nominated Off-Broadway actress, modern dance teacher, orchestra conductor, and college professor; the list goes on and on.

While Angelou's story is an extraordinary one, the power of having hopes, goals, and dreams can be found in everyday examples all around us. The hope of a championship season gives a football player the will to get through two-a-days in the heat of August. The dream of becoming a positive influence on a child's life drives teachers and educators. The goal of getting healthy and losing weight gives a person the motivation to skip the cheesecake and spend an extra 20 minutes on the treadmill. The dream of a normal life gives an addict the push through rehab and the drive to make the conscious decision not to use. The Bible is filled with Scriptures that relate to the power of hope. The casino industry, and state lotteries, too, are entire industries that play upon people's hopes of striking it big.

And science even suggests that hope can heal. Think about the well-documented placebo effect: Study after study reports that patients who are given a sugar pill or other form of inactive substance in place of real medication often report feeling better.

Swimming Toward The Light

A story in *The Light*, a book by author and journalist Mike Evans, illustrates that the power of hope is biological, too. Evans describes a group of scientists who performed an experiment using rats, aiming to uncover how outside factors affected their will to live.[2]

One rat was placed in a large tub of water with sides high enough to prevent it from getting out. In addition, the room was pitch black. The researchers timed how long the rat would keep swimming before it gave up. The creature struggled for a little more than three minutes before giving up.

In the next part of the experiment, the researchers placed another rat in the same tub of water. But this time, they placed a bright light into the room. The second rat swam for more than 36 hours – that's 700 times longer than the rat with no light.

The reason for that determination? The second rat literally saw the light at the end of the tub. In other words, it had hope, a reason to keep swimming.

It's the same with humans. Without hope, without a light to move toward and focus on, we flail about in the tub of life like, well, a drowning rat in the darkness.

Building Hope → Becoming a Leader

So what does hope have to do with being a leader, you ask? They go hand in hand. Good leaders possess the ability to inspire hope in others. Leaders choose to focus not on the struggles and challenges of today, but rather the better things that lie ahead when we overcome those struggles and challenges.

Good leaders possess the ability to inspire hope in others. Remember, under our concept of Leadership Redefined, you don't have to be a leader anywhere near the level of an Obama or a Churchill or an Angelou for the power of hope to have a worthy function in your life. Good leaders at all levels – from powerful political leaders to middle managers to the individual contributors in an organization – are adept at this: honing their vision, and their actions, toward a positive outcome.

But it's hard to have hope for something when you don't know what that something is. Which brings us back to the essence of this chapter: Why is it so critical to extract a dream, a goal, or a target? The answer: because a dream, goal, or target defines and clarifies what you're putting your hopes on and working toward. It's a catalyst for fulfillment, enrichment, and enhancement of your life. Certainly, you can have a fulfilled, enriched, enhanced life without ever setting a goal. But consider for a minute how good things could really be if you did? In other words, goals help you become your best self.

Hit The Target

Before I ever introduce this topic during presentations at conferences or to organizations, I have a favorite exercise that clearly illustrates the importance of extracting a goal, a dream, or a target.

Well into the presentation, I ask for three volunteers to come help me run a group simulation in the front of the room. A twitchy silence usually takes over as the audience members avoid eye contact with me and encourage their neighbor to volunteer.

After a few moments, though, the extrovert in the crowd *(there's always at least one)* pops out of their chair, and I have my first volunteer. Then, when all three have assembled with me on stage, I thank them for volunteering and assign them roles as Contestants 1, 2, and 3 for the exercise. I instruct them to then wait outside until someone comes to get them.

Once they're gone, I congratulate the rest of the crowd for not volunteering, and I tell them that I'm going to "mess with" the three contestants. This makes them even gladder they didn't volunteer and excited to see what fate is in store for the brave souls who did.

Before I bring the contestants back, though, I give the rest of the crowd an assignment: to observe the contestants, try to imagine what they must be thinking and feeling, record their observations, and, finally, jot down what *they themselves* would be thinking and feeling if *they* were up front doing the simulation with me.

Once the crowd is clear on their assignment, I have Contestant 1 escorted into the room. The crowd has been instructed to applaud like crazy when he or she walks in; think rock star reception here. (The applause has nothing to do with the actual exercise; it just makes the contestants more uncomfortable, which is so deliciously fun.)

The exercise starts when I say to the first contestant: "If I had a ball right now – a baseball or football or basketball – I would give it to you. But since I don't, I am going to simply wad up this piece of paper and give it to you. I want you to pretend this piece of paper is a ball and all I want you to do with it is THROW IT AND HIT THE TARGET."

A goal defines and clarifies what you're putting your hopes on and working toward.

I hand the contestant the balled-up paper and then immediately turn my back and walk away, leaving the poor soul all alone on the stage in front of the group.

The reactions from participants at this point are all over the place. Some start looking around the stage for a target. Some ask questions to the crowd, who have been instructed not to answer. Some just stand there, motionless. After a few agonizing seconds of this, the audience usually begins to snicker.

Some try to ask me questions, looking to get clarification. From the side of the stage where I am lurking, I merely repeat what I have already told them, "Throw the ball. Hit the target." And again, I duck into the periphery.

Put yourself in the contestant's shoes for a moment. How would you be feeling?

Stupid? Awkward? Uncomfortable? Angry? Resentful? Confused? Set up? Tricked?

From here, the reactions of the contestants vary wildly. Some refuse to throw the paper ball. Others throw it at the crowd. The more aggressive types sometimes sling a paper fastball right at my head. No matter what they do, I thank them, tell them they handled the situation perfectly, and have the crowd applaud for them. As the contestant heads back to their seat, I remind the audience of their assignment and to record their observations and thoughts.

The exact same process is repeated with Contestant 2.

By the time the third contestant is escorted in, the crowd is really into it, eager to see how the final victim – er, *contestant* – will handle the uncertainty of the assignment. But with Contestant 3, I change things up just a bit. Upon handing over the paper ball and giving the instructions to "Hit the target," this time I turn on the LCD projector, and a giant image of a target appears on the screen in front of the room.

What happens next is as predictable as the sun rising in the east: The audience is shocked; Contestants 1 and 2 are seriously ticked off; and Contestant 3 immediately turns, throws the paper ball, hits the target and looks at me as if to say, *"That's it? That was easy. What took the others so long to do that?"*

Put yourself in the contestant's shoes. How would you be feeling?

As the audience once again records their own observations of what just transpired and Contestant 3 heads back to their seat, I mention that while the exercise was easy for them, I did not give the first two contestants a target to throw at.

Now it is time for the crowd to report on their observations. I ask them to share what words they jotted down with respect to the first two contestants' experience. Invariably they use words and descriptions like:

- Confused
- Hesitant
- Don't know what is expected
- Angry
- Not sure what to do
- Tricked
- Why did I volunteer?
- Set up
- Why won't Dave answer my questions?
- I'll get him back for this!
- I'll just make up something
- When will this be over?
- Doing anything is better than just standing here

Next, I have the audience generate a list of observations revolving around Contestant 3. This list tends to include the following:

- This is easy
- I can do this
- Man/woman of action
- No hesitation
- Confident
- Knows what is expected
- Clear understanding of the desired outcome
- Skills and resources to accomplish the assignment

After the two lists have been generated by the audience, everyone is finally ready to hear what in the world this has to do with anything! (Remember, I still have not introduced the principle of Extract a Goal to the group, just the exercise.) Here are the two key questions – and the whole idea behind all of this craziness:

1. Guess how you tend to feel when there is no clear goal, or when you're not sure what the target is? (The answer is found in the list of observations made about Contestants 1 and 2.)

2. Guess how you tend to feel when there is a clear goal, when you know what the target is? (This time, the answer is found in the list of observations about Contestant 3.)

In order to have any chance of hitting the target, or reaching the goal, you have to know what you are aiming for. What you should hit. What you are putting your time, energy, and attention toward.

In order to have any chance of hitting the target, or reaching the goal, you have to know what you are aiming for.

In other words, you have to know what the goal is. Just like the old saying, "Men and rivers seldom drift to success," you need to identify where you want to arrive. Only then you can align your activities, energy, and effort in that direction – toward success, in other words.

American leadership guru Peter Drucker puts it this way: "The best way to predict the future is to create it." Or as another well-known life coach, Stephen Covey, says, "Begin with the end in mind."

Five Ways Goals Can Enrich Your Life

Generally speaking, leaders have experienced the power behind these five principles.

1. Goals help you clarify and concentrate your efforts.

We'll talk more about this in Chapter 4, Exchange Non-Essentials, but for now, think of a time when you knew you had to leave the house for an important trip: perhaps a business conference, or a vacation with your family. Your to-do list is overflowing with tasks, but – with that final, must-be-out-the-door deadline driving it all – how freakishly efficiently can you work your way through that list? I know on days like that, I'm able to accomplish far more than I normally do.

This is what goals do for your life on a larger scale – they enable you to cut the fluff and zero in on what you need to do to reach your desired outcome. When you Extract a Goal or Target, you are more able to identify next steps and take action that will get you closer to it, especially when you come to forks in the road. Life doesn't travel along a straight path, as we all know; instead, it's a series of forks. And when you've crystallized or clarified where you want to go – what kind of a parent or professional or manager or student you want to be, how you want to perform a job – choosing the best option or which fork in the road you'll follow becomes almost natural, like a gut instinct that you need to tune into.

> *Goals enable you to cut the fluff and zero in on what you need to do to reach your desired outcome.*

For example, if the goal you have identified is "I want to eat healthier," then you can bet that life will throw all kinds of forks at you *(pun very much intended)*. Every time you open the refrigerator door, every time you open up a menu, every time you take a break at work – forks come flying at you. To the degree that you have Extracted a Goal, it becomes easier to identify the option that will get you closer to the achievement of that goal.

Ideally, that makes it a little easier to know you need to choose grapes over chips, and carrots over cookies. And it becomes easier to identify which action or reactions will take you further away from your goal.

Maybe your goal is "I want to get better at using technology at work." The fork may show up on Saturday morning, shrouded in those cozy blankets and pillows in your bed. Do you sleep in, or do you attend the free social media class you signed up for? A clear target – understanding, once and for all, what the heck Twitter is all about and how those crazy # and @ symbols can actually serve a purpose for your business, for example – helps you make decisions that are in line with where you want to go, making it easier to set the alarm clock and resist the temptation of the snooze button.

2. Goals help you see your progress, which helps you progress even further.

Let's say you have a goal of running a half-marathon, but you've never run more than five miles at a stretch. So you set up a running calendar and start ticking off your mileage as you reach it. After a few initial runs of five miles, you add on another half-mile, then another, and another, and before you know it, you're up to 10 miles – double digits! It's an incredible feeling to make progress on purpose, which in turn motivates you to the next milestone in your journey.

The well-known radio talk show host and financial whiz Dave Ramsey bases his famous get-out-of-debt philosophy on this concept. He teaches people to simply list their debts from smallest to largest. Then he instructs his audience to throw all their extra effort and money at the smallest one. Once it's paid off, attention turns to the next debt on the list by applying the same amount of money to it. The idea is that by first knocking out the smallest debt or challenge, people begin to see and feel progress, which only inspires them to keep on going toward the next hurdle.

3. Goals help you develop more self-confidence.

It's humanly impossible to achieve a goal you've set for yourself and not feel better about yourself. Enough said.

4. Goals help you become proactive, not reactive.

Goals make us accountable and call attention to our inactivity. When we're focused on achieving our goals, we're moving forward and progressing, intentionally, no matter what life throws at us. Conversely, without goals, it's much easier to drift along and become susceptible to outside influences: the remote control, Facebook, that bad-influence friend who always gets you into trouble, or just one more game of Angry Birds.

5. Goals help you recognize opportunities.

Similar to the way in which goals help clarify the path to take, goals also help us open our eyes to the ways in which our environment, surroundings, people, and situations can boost us toward achievement. With a clear goal in mind, it's easier to recognize an opportunity that might be hidden, or a contact that could help, or any of the other subtle ways that the universe can reach out with a helping hand. (There's serious science behind this stuff; read on to find out what it is.)

The Fascinating Science Behind Goal-Setting

Perhaps more people would set goals if they understood the fascinating science that demonstrates the effectiveness of goal setting. It involves a tangle of neurons at the base of your brain called the reticular activating system, or RAS. This network of brain cells has several varied functions: regulating sleep and waking up, walking, and the ability to consciously focus your attention on something. The RAS is the automatic mechanism inside your brain that brings relevant information to your attention.

Some researchers describe it as the bridge between our consciousness and subconsciousness. It serves this function by acting as the ultimate spam filter for the constant stream of stimuli that bombard our senses every minute of every day. Without the RAS, we'd go bonkers under a tsunami of sensory information. And therein lies one of the RAS's most important capabilities with respect to developing leadership skills: It can be a critical ally in achieving our goals and dreams. Why? Because, once you clearly and specifically define what you want – when you Extract a Goal, Dream, or Target – the RAS homes in on information, resources, and stimuli that relate to that end result.

To illustrate the RAS at work, consider for a minute the feeling you get when you walk through a spider web. You flick it aside, only to feel for the next few minutes that an entire nest of arachnids is taking a crochet class on your entire epidermis. That feeling is your RAS leaping into action. Since noticing that first silken thread, the nerve receptors in your skin keep sending stimuli to your RAS, which let it know to be on the lookout for similar

Consider the feeling you get when you walk through a spider web.

sensory info. The next thing you know, you're squirming and wiggling and brushing perceived cobwebs off your body like a madman (or woman).

Research suggests that the RAS lets in only two specific types of stimuli: that which presents an immediate threat (there could be an actual spider in that cobweb, for example), and that which presents value. The latter is critical for our purposes: When we Extract a Goal and define, clearly and specifically, what we want to do, achieve, or become, it's like we flip a switch in our RAS to become attuned to information specific to that goal. Think of it this way: Remember that childhood game called "Punchbug" or "Spudbug" that you'd play with your siblings on a long car trip, slugging the heck out of each other when either of you saw a Volkswagen Beetle? When you weren't playing the game, those round little cars were almost invisible, but once the game was on and you were actively looking for them, you'd see them everywhere.

Same goes at the airport, for example. As a frequent traveler, I spend a lot of time in airports, and as any other road warrior can probably identify with, I pretty much zone out when I'm moving through bustling terminals. Except, that is, when I hear my flight being called over the loudspeaker, snapping my subconscious to conscious attention thanks to the efforts of my RAS.

In this way, when we bring our conscious attention to a goal, dream, or target, we can actively program our RAS. Once that happens, you begin noticing and experiencing things that may have been there all along – a friend of a friend in a career field you want to transition into, for example, or a gym just a few streets away where you can jump-start your training for your first triathlon.

With that in mind, isn't it fair then to say that we have more control of some of the things that we describe as "just meant to be" that happen as soon as we commit to a goal, dream, or target than we tend to think?

Absolutely, I believe. And the potential to achieve some of our greatest life dreams lies in that little bundle of nerves at the base of our brain; that is, if we take the initiative to harness its power by Extracting a Goal.

Goal-Setting Done Right

I would be remiss if I didn't mention someone whom I consider a great example in terms of his life goals: Billy Graham. Regardless of where you fall on the spiritual spectrum, it's hard to argue with his accomplishments. In my mind, he's a prime example of someone who lived his life with a clear goal: to be as closely connected to God as possible and to introduce others to Him.

Born Nov. 7, 1918 as William Franklin Graham, he became one of the most well-respected religious icons in our country, transcending religion and gaining widespread popularity for his sincerity, compassion, and wisdom. Not once in his incredible career, during which several presidents have sought his consultation, has he engaged in any of the scandals that taint many people's perceptions of evangelists. No surprise, then, that Graham has frequently been honored in surveys, including "Greatest Living American," and has consistently ranked among the most admired persons in the United States and the world.

About 10 years ago, community leaders in Charlotte, North Carolina, invited their city's "Favorite Son" to a luncheon honoring him. Battling the effects of Parkinson's disease, the

81-year-old Graham, who never liked to chase the spotlight, was hesitant to accept, but he finally agreed.

After lunch and a series of speakers praising him, Graham humbly stepped to the podium, looked at the crowd and said, "I'm reminded today of Albert Einstein, the great physicist who this month has been honored by *Time Magazine* as the Man of the Century."

He continued with a well-known anecdote about Einstein:

As the wild-haired astrophysicist was once traveling by train from Princeton, New Jersey, the conductor came down the aisle, punching passengers' tickets. When he came to Einstein, the great man reached into his vest and trouser pockets, but he pulled out no ticket. He then looked in his briefcase – still, no ticket. It wasn't in the seat beside him, either.

The conductor said, "Dr. Einstein, I know who you are. We all know who you are. I'm sure you bought a ticket. Don't worry about it."

Einstein nodded appreciatively. The conductor continued punching tickets down the aisle, and as he was about to move to the next car, he noticed Einstein down on his hands and knees, searching under his seat.

The conductor rushed back and said, "Dr. Einstein, please don't worry, I know who you are. You don't need a ticket. I'm sure you bought one."

Einstein looked at him and said, "Young man, I too, know who I am. What I don't know is where I'm going."

Always the master of timing, Graham paused as the audience chuckled at that final line. Then Graham continued his story:

See the suit I'm wearing? It's a brand-new suit. My children and grandchildren tell me I've gotten a little slovenly in my old age. I used to be a bit more fastidious. So I went out and bought a new suit for this luncheon and one more occasion.

You know what that occasion is? This is the suit in which I'll be buried. But when you hear the news that I'm dead, I don't want you to immediately remember the suit I'm wearing. I want you to remember this: I not only know who I am, I also know where I'm going.

But What If I Feel Like Einstein?

But what if, unlike Billy Graham, you're feeling more like Einstein, scrambling around on the floor of the train looking for his ticket? What if you, too, feel a little lost about where you're headed on this train called life?

First of all, try not to sweat it so much. Society bombards us with messages that not-so-subtly say we should be striving for grandiose (and often, unrealistic) goals like having mega-wealth or supermodel looks or being the type of parent who not only holds down a successful career but has enough time to make her kids organic meals from scratch, oh, and by the way, looks like Kelly Ripa while she's doing it. Forget that. Goals don't have to be earth-shattering or life-changing. They can be as simple as learning to play the guitar. Or finding a job that, while it may not ever make you a millionaire, makes you happy most of the time. Or making time for morning exercise. Or, in my case, watching a game with my son once a week.

A goal can be defined as something that you'd like to do, accomplish, or achieve.

In other words, a goal can be defined as something that you'd like to do, accomplish, or achieve. And if you really want to get a gold star in the process, go broader than just one area. Consider what author Jack Canfield suggests in his superb book

The Success Principles: How to Get From Where You Are to Where You Want to Be, and set goals across several aspects of your life: financial; job/career; physical health; spiritual; relationships; personal development; and community.

Do you feel fulfilled and satisfied with one area, but completely off track in another?

Take a long, hard look at your life with respect to these categories. Are any of them lacking? Does one overpower another? Do you feel fulfilled and satisfied with one area, but completely off track in another? Taking a look at your answers is an excellent exercise in taking stock of your life.

Another Approach: Considering The Opposite

Another alternative that can help you clarify your goals: Try a little technique I use sometimes involving opposites. In other words, try to visualize what you *don't* want out of life, in all its various aspects, from personal to professional to spiritual. That could be affirmations like the following:

- I don't want a nagging, critical relationship with my partner
- I don't want to be so tired in the evening that I can't play with my children
- I don't want to live in a cardboard box on the street, at the mercy of handouts from passersby
- I don't want to continue working in a job that doesn't fulfill me
- I don't want an unhealthy, sedentary lifestyle
- I don't want to be so intimidated by technology

Now, just flip those to discover the hidden goals within:

- I want a positive, loving relationship with my partner
- I want to have enough energy in the evening to play with my kids
- I want to live in a nice home or apartment and be able to support myself
- I want to work in a job or career that fulfills me
- I want an active lifestyle
- I want to be able to tweet and text with confidence, so I can at least pretend to keep up with my children's lives

See? You're already on your way.

Rewards From Within

No matter what your goal is, though, there's an important element to consider with respect to goals: the intrinsic rewards they offer. An intrinsic reward is one that comes from within; it's that warm, delicious feeling that spreads through your soul when you're doing something you truly enjoy, or something that's truly good for you and your well-being. Extrinsic rewards, by contrast, are the feel-good vibes we get when somebody else recognizes our accomplishment or achievement. While intrinsic rewards come from within, extrinsic rewards come from an external source.

So why is it so important to consider whether your goal has intrinsic, rather than extrinsic, rewards? Because, in order to be a good leader, you must be driven from within. In fact, a great measure of leadership is choosing to do the right thing knowing that no one may ever discover it or recognize you for it. If you are living your life looking to others to validate who you are and what you are doing, you're living a losing proposition for a couple of reasons. The first is that many people spend most of their time thinking about themselves; in other words, people generally (and sadly) don't spend their days looking for ways to encourage, affirm, express thanks or gratitude, or build up those around them. By contrast, people today seem to be far more critical of others than ever before.

The second reason is that, no matter where you are in life, there will always be others who have more than you, and others who have less than you, in terms of material wealth, looks, or job success. While competition can serve as a helpful motivator, constantly wondering how you measure up to those around you can zap critical time and energy that you could be focusing on yourself. Leaders realize this is a critical aspect to making progress: We can't live our lives waiting for others to prop us up with validation.

We can't live our lives waiting for others to prop us up with validation.

The Express Soccer Team

Fresh out of college, single, and employed with a company car and an expense account, I felt like I had arrived in the world. Everything was going my way, so it was time to think about someone other than myself. But where to plug in? What kind of volunteer work would I enjoy and would be meaningful not only to me, but also to others?

I decided the YMCA would be a good place for me. I was an All-Conference NCAA Division 1 soccer player at Mercer University (go Bears!), and surely I could help coach a team.

When I inquired at the Y, they asked me what age group I wanted to work with and I really didn't care. I figured I could teach the older kids some of the more advanced aspects of the game, but the younger kids I could help by getting them started with some solid foundations upon which their skill could really take off. Either way, it sounded like fun.

The Y said they had the perfect team for me: The Express. And, instead of being an assistant to some father coaching his kid's team, I was given head coaching duties of this team: a group of 12-and-under boys whose previous coach had abruptly left right after the last season was over. *Who would do that?* I thought.

I quickly learned why. This team was awful! No discipline. No skill. No desire. Instead, they whined and complained constantly. After the first practice, I was starting to doubt my decision to take over this team.

But then I remembered my coach when I was 12. He didn't have a kid on the team, either. He just loved soccer and wanted to teach us to love it too. I remember thinking how cool this guy was, and it dawned on me that I could be "that" coach for these kids.

Pouring myself into these kids became my passion. I developed practice drills, exercises, and games to teach and reinforce skills they would need in a real match. We started to have a great time at practice. I was thrilled to see these guys start to really come along.

Then came our first game.

We lost.

So I started coming early to practice with those who could get there early. I began staying late to work with those who could stay late.

We lost a few more games.

I developed what in the coaching industry are sometimes known as IDPs –individual development plans – for each player and implemented them.

We lost again.

I started meeting with each player individually to point out areas where they could hone their skills at home.

We lost some more games.

Oh, but then one magnificent Saturday morning, The Express won! Not a forfeit from the other team, mind you, but a *real victory* – 1-0! I was on top of the world.

But not because any of the players thanked me after the game. Because they didn't. Neither did any of the players' parents, or a referee, or anybody at the YMCA who knew of the team's woes in previous seasons.

No, I did not receive one mention of gratitude from anyone about that hard-earned victory.

And did it matter? Not one bit.

No one thanked me or rewarded me. No one recognized or acknowledged my role in the team's victory and how hard I'd worked to help the team earn it. Yet I was not one bit concerned. All I cared about was that the team won. *And it felt great!*

Extracting a Dream helps build a self-motivated desire for results, regardless of the encouragement (or lack there of) from others.

That glorious feeling was the beauty and power of an intrinsic reward: *It all came from within.*

Which brings us back to the power of Extracting a Dream, Goal, or Target: It helps build a self-motivated desire for results, regardless of the encouragement (or lack thereof) from others.

The Holstee Manifesto

In mid-2009, a group of Brooklyn-based entrepreneurs had experienced limited success selling their eco-friendly, responsibly manufactured clothing, mostly to family and friends who were supporting them. The trio felt very hopeful about their endeavor and decided to quit their full-time jobs to pursue their dream. In those heady first days after quitting, they had no real idea where they were heading as a company. All they knew was that they were full of crackling energy, ideas, and inspiration.

So the three founders sat down on the steps of Union Square in Manhattan and wrote down exactly what they were thinking. The process wasn't about sales, service, or other jargon-y terms like team effort. Instead, they tapped into how they wanted to live their lives – and how they wanted to create a company in line with that vision. It was, as they say on their website, "a reminder of what we live for."

If you don't like something, change it. If you don't like your job, quit. If you don't have enough time, stop watching TV.

The result of that session became known as The Holstee Manifesto, and it became not only the company's motto but also a viral sensation. Since posting it to their website, the company, Holstee, estimates the message has been shared nearly half a million times and viewed more than 60 million times online.

Here's how it reads:

This is your LIFE. Do what you love, and do it often.
If you don't like something, change it.
If you don't like your job, quit.
If you don't have enough time, stop watching TV.

> *If you are looking for the love of your life,*
> *stop; they will be waiting for you when*
> *you start doing things you love.*
> *Stop over-analyzing, LIFE IS SIMPLE. All*
> *emotions are beautiful.*
> *When you eat, appreciate every last bite.*
> *Open your mind, arms, and heart to new things*
> *and people, we are united in our differences.*
> *Ask the next person you see what their passion*
> *is, and share your inspiring dream with them.*
> *TRAVEL OFTEN; getting lost will help you*
> *find yourself.*
> *Some opportunities come only once; seize them.*
> *Life is about the people you meet, and the things*
> *you create with them, so go out and start creating.*
> *LIFE IS SHORT. Live your dream*
> *and wear your passion.*

Pretty powerful, huh? Can you imagine how different the corporate world – and the world in general, for that matter – would be if every company had a mission statement like that?

Express Your Vision To Others

For the founders of Holstee, just having those core values about life wasn't enough. The Holstee Manifesto illustrates a critical aspect of Extracting a Dream: Express Your Vision to Others. It's part of the action component to making progress.

Something transformational takes place when you articulate your vision.

In order to fully internalize something, we have to vocalize it. Indeed, something transformational takes place when you articulate your vision to the world:

- It seals your commitment
- It invites accountability
- It galvanizes resolve
- And, as in the case of Holstee, it can open new doors: Sales of posters and T-shirts printed with the manifesto became an unexpected revenue stream for the company.

Most importantly, though, when we Express Our Vision to Others it is amazing to watch them line up behind us to help us get there.

When I finally made the decision to write my first book, *Sticks & Stones Exposed: The Power of Our Words,* I didn't tell anyone. I was afraid I would fail and then still have to answer all the questions about when it was coming out, how it was going, and who was going to publish it.

While the goal was clearly articulated in my mind – to publish a book – I

> *When we Express Our Vision to Others it is amazing to watch them line up behind us to help us get there.*

felt like I was in way over my head. I didn't know how to find a publisher, design a cover, find out if my working title had ever been used before, how to get an ISBN number, how to get a Library of Congress number, and so many other details. It seemed every day I discovered yet another aspect about which I had no clue.

It was overwhelming and disheartening, and my not-even-launched book project slowed to a frozen snail's pace.

Finally, I got fed up with myself, and the desire to get moving on this dream overrode my trepidation. I whispered my vision to another person. They got all excited about my project and referred me to someone who knew about book cover design who knew someone who had a publisher friend who knew someone who had written a book. The domino effect was in full swing. It seemed the more I Expressed My Vision to Others, the more people I met who were excited to help me accomplish my dream.

And guess what – I finished that book (you can read the first chapter at the end of this book), and even went along to write another, which you're holding in your hands right now.

Identifying Goals: Not Just For New Year's

So, when is the best time to identify a goal, a dream, a target? The most common time seems to be at the end of one year and the beginning of another. Annually, millions of people look at this window of time as the perfect moment to create New Year's resolutions. These resolutions, though, are truly nothing more than new goals or targets that we want to achieve, or recycled goals from years past that we have yet to accomplish.

Anything really worth starting is worth starting whenever you want.

But sadly, by the end of January, most of us have already abandoned our New Year's resolutions and feel like failures again. In fact, according to the latest numbers from neuroscience research, up to 88 percent of all resolutions end in failure. (Bad habits are hard to break, and they're almost impossible if we try to break them all at once.)

And who says resolutions are only to be set once a year, on January 1st? Whose big idea was that? I mean, anything really worth starting is worth starting whenever you want to start.

You can pick any day – the first day of a new month, or a new week, or even a new day – to Extract a Dream, Goal, or Target for yourself. There are no limits on when you should start fresh in reaching a new aspiration for your life.

So why not now?

EXPLORE ON YOUR OWN

1. Think back to your childhood. What were the circumstances or influences that helped shape your hopes and dreams for the future?

2. In your life right now, how does hope in the future bring power to your present?

3. Name some ways you can inspire hope in others.

4. Identify a past goal you set for yourself and think about how you attained or achieved it. Describe how you felt when you succeeded.

5. Describe a time when a having a goal helped you clarify and concentrate your efforts.

6. In your job, why is important to be driven from within and be able to celebrate intrinsic rewards?

7. Think about an experience in your life when you did something really positive and no one noticed it or thanked you for doing it. Describe what you did and how you felt.

8. Describe a time when you Expressed Your Vision to Others and the role those others played in helping you.

9. Have you ever asked your [spouse/significant other/colleague/boss] about a shared goal you could achieve together? If not, why, and when will you do this?

10. Who could you share a goal, dream or target with? When will you do that?

11. Since goals are critical in helping us make progress on purpose, take the time to identify some goals in your life. Rather than thinking of them in a broad sense, which can be overwhelming (i.e., what are your life goals?), look at the individual areas of your life and identify goals for each area:

- Professional
- Financial
- Physical/Health
- Family
- Social/Relationships
- Spiritual
- Personal Development

CHAPTER 3
EXAMINE EVERYTHING

People only see what they are prepared to see.
- Ralph Waldo Emerson

A man is crossing the U.S. border on his bicycle. He has two big bags on his shoulders. The Border Control guard asks him, "What's in the bags?"

He replies, "Sand."

The guard says, "Take them off – we'll examine them."

The man takes the two bags off and the guard thoroughly searches them, finding nothing but sand. The fellow puts the bags back on his shoulders, and proceeds to cross the border on his bicycle.

Two weeks later, the same scene unfolds, with the same man crossing the border on his bike, two heavy bags on his shoulders.

"What have you got there?" the Border Patrol officer asks the man.

"Sand," he replies.

"Take them off, we'll examine them."

Every few weeks for several months, this scenario unfolded. One week, however, the sand-toting fellow didn't show up. Off duty one day, the guard ran into him in a small U.S. town just over the border.

The guard says, "Buddy, you had us pulling our hair out! We knew you were smuggling something. But we just couldn't figure out what. You have my word that I won't get you in trouble, but I have to know –what were you bringing in anyway?"

Smiling, the smuggler answers, "Bicycles."[3]

Watching Your Watch

The basic principle behind Examining Everything is like a grown-up application of a safety message that was drilled into our heads as kids before we crossed the street: Stop, look, and listen. However, Examining Everything means that we must do each of those steps with a far greater depth and intensity than simply glancing down the street for traffic and tuning our ears for the sounds of an oncoming car.

Research conducted by Bullova, one of the world's leading watch manufacturers, indicates that we tend to look at our watches approximately 40 times a day. So *surely* we all know what our watches look like, right?

Wrong. So wrong, in fact, that I decided to prove it with some audience members in a presentation to a large group of senior managers in a Fortune 500 company. I decided to conduct an informal survey with this group, which was, understandably, full of Type-A personalities. I asked the people who were wearing wristwatches with faces on them to stand, put the arm with the watch behind their backs, and answer, to themselves, four simple questions about their watch to see which manager in the room was the most observant.

With a group of overachievers like this, you could tell each one was gunning to beat their fellow managers.

With a group of overachievers like this, you could tell each one was gunning to beat their fellow managers. The room virtually hummed with the buzz of adrenaline and competition as they awaited the questions:

- **Question 1:** What color is the face of your watch? (Group collective consensus: *Come on, this is kid stuff!! I've had this watch forever!*)
- **Question 2:** How many hands does your watch have? *(Oh, that's easy enough ... Two, I'm pretty sure.)*
- **Question 3:** What color are the hands of your watch? *(Hmmm. Errr. Black-uhhh-silver? Is that right? Now that I think about it, I'm not positive...)*
- **Question 4:** How are the hours on your watch delineated: Roman numerals or Arabic? Do *all* the hours have numbers? If not, how are the others marked? Dashes? Diamonds? Dots? A combination of all those? *(&$#!)*

Even from the stage, I could see brows starting to furrow and sweat starting to bead as we did the countdown to looking at their watches. Groans erupted throughout the room as scores of managers took their seats, having answered incorrectly.

When the dust had settled about 12 people were still standing, meaning they had answered all four questions correctly, and I had the audience give them a round of applause. They stood tall and proud, reveling in their superior observation skills and the affirmation of their colleagues.

That was about to change, and the real fun was about to begin.

As the applause died down, I looked at the remaining dozen and said, "I don't believe you. Truth be told, I think you are lying. In fact, I am going to personally come down there and check your answers for myself."

The crowd went nuts, whooping and hollering like they were in the audience of a South Georgia catfish toss. And indeed, when I began to check their watches, the first three victims, er, *audience members,* I'd chosen had gotten at least one question wrong about basic characteristics of their watches.

A man named Ron, however, was by far the most animated, a real live wire. I took his watch so he couldn't see it, and we flew through the first three questions as Ron's confidence soared. We came to the fourth and final question. This was it. If he nailed this answer, he'd clearly come out on top of what had turned into a very competitive exercise.

When I asked how the hours were identified, Ron stated, "Roman numerals! All 12 of them!"

"Wanna bet?" I asked. (Keep in mind *I am holding his watch and looking at its face.*)

"I'll bet you a thousand dollars!" he hollered.

"Ok, let me make sure I've got this right," I responded. "You are willing to bet me a *thousand dollars* that your watch has all 12 numbers on it, and they are all Roman numerals?"

"Yes, I am!" Ron replied, puffing his chest like a peacock on steroids. "What's the matter? Afraid to bet me?" He was really hamming it up for the crowd, which made me savor even more what was about to unfold.

Humans are the only creatures who can deceive themselves.

I turned his watch over so he could see it and asked him, "Do you see a 12?"

The place went into an uproar as Ron stared at me, disbelieving, as he saw his watch manufacturer's logo instead of a 12. As the noise died down, I added,

"How about a three?" (There was no three but rather a small window with the date.)

As the laughter started up again, Ron explained that his watch had been a gift from his father, and it was one of his most cherished possessions. He then added, "I can't believe I have looked at it all these years and never *really* seen it before today."

A Quote To Remember

The anecdote about the bicycle smuggler and Ron's story – and believe me, that was a moment to remember for both of us, but for different reasons – are real-life examples that illustrate one of my favorite quotes from my father. I've heard him say it more than all the others combined, and it sums up his modus operandi throughout an incredible life:

> *"Examine everything carefully and hold fast to that which is good."*[4]

It is a simple and yet profound truth. It means that we should constantly take a survey of our lives – Examine Everything – and hang onto only the things that are positive. If we dig a little deeper, we can find within in it a call to honesty: with ourselves, with others, with what we observe – or *think* we observe – in the world around us.

You see, we humans are the only creatures who can deceive themselves. In fact, we're great at it. We can fool ourselves into oblivion – about how good we are at something, about how well our business is performing, about the details of our watch, about any number of issues in which we undeservedly give ourselves or others the benefit of the doubt, without ever truly taking the time to uncover and understand the reality. In fact, just to show you how good we are at self-deceit and self-deception, and how capable we are in believing what we want to believe without close examination, let me share with you an old story.

The Slap Heard 'Round The Train Car

Many decades ago, a passenger train was pulling out of the station in a small Eastern European town. Four travelers shared a cozy compartment: an American grandmother, her beautiful 24-year-old granddaughter, a Nazi officer in uniform, and a Romanian officer, also in uniform.

Each of the passengers knew a smattering of language, so the conversation was light, mostly focusing on the beautiful landscape and the weather. Everyone seemed to be enjoying themselves.

After traveling through the scenic countryside for some time, the train entered a long, dark tunnel, throwing the compartment into pitch-black darkness. The railroad car went silent as the blackness seemed to close in on them. Then out of the quiet came the distinct sound of a kiss, followed by a hearty slap. Moments later the train exited the tunnel.

No one said a word. But everyone knew – or *thought* they knew – what had happened.

Then out of the quiet came the distinct sound of a kiss, followed by a hearty slap.

The American grandmother sat tall and proud in her seat, thinking: *"What a fine young woman I have raised. My granddaughter will be able to take care of herself in this cruel world. I am so proud of her!"* You see Grandma knew, in her mind, what had happened: that one of the soldiers had tried to get fresh with her granddaughter.

Next to her sat her stunned granddaughter. *"WOW! That sounded like Grandma packed quite a wallop!"* she mused, looking at her grandmother with new admiration. *"But I'm surprised she would get so upset that one of these fellas tried to steal a kiss. They seem nice enough and they certainly are handsome in their uniforms. Still, I gotta hand it to Grandma!"* You see, the granddaughter knew in her mind exactly what happened.

Across from the granddaughter, the Nazi sat rubbing his face, fuming, *"Oh how clever those Romanians are. They steal a kiss and get the other guy slapped. I will have my revenge when we exit this train."* He surely knew – and felt – what had happened.

In the other corner of the train car, the Romanian sat quietly chuckling to himself. *"That was absolutely priceless. I kiss the back of my own hand and then get to slap the Nazi!"*

All four people *believed* they knew exactly what had happened, yet 75 percent of them were wrong! Indeed, three of those four passengers experienced an example of the wise words of Aesop, who said, "Appearances are often deceiving."

The Missing Teachers

In case you don't envision yourself traveling on a European train with a Nazi anytime soon, consider this real-life, modern-day scenario that illustrates the same self-deception in effect.

It happened with a principal from a school in the Southeast I was working with a few years ago. We spent one morning observing different classrooms during the transitional time when her school district, like many others across the country, was in the process of "mainstreaming" the students with special needs into the general education population. As a part of the process, the special education teachers were now working side-by-side, in the same room, with the general education teachers. I wanted to see how these teachers would perform sharing a classroom when they had, for years, had a room all to themselves.

After seeing four classrooms, we headed to the cafeteria. On the way, I asked about the effect of the recent reduction in force that her school's district had experienced.

"It's devastating!" the principal said. "It was so painful to let some of our teachers go. We have just barely enough to cover all the students and with the changes in standards and increases in student achievement, I really need everyone at the top of their game."

"Wow," I said. "How are you ever going to do it with four fewer teachers?"

"What do you mean?" she asked, surprised. "What are you talking about?"

"Well, let's back up a second. Tell me what you just saw in those four classrooms this morning," I responded.

"Ok," she said. "I saw two teachers in each room sharing the responsibility of teaching both the general ed and the special ed students at the same time. They were communicating, collaborating, and sharing best practices to help the students of varying ability to learn the material."

"Is that the plan?" I asked. "Is that what they are supposed to do?"

"Yes," the principal replied. "We have been working very hard as a faculty to develop a professional learning community where the teachers work side-by-side co-teaching simultaneously."

"Well," I said, "that's not exactly what I observed."

"It's not?!" The principal was shocked. "What did you see?"

"I saw *one* teacher in each room actually *teaching* and another adult, who appeared to be their mentor, helping the teacher teach all the students," I explained. "Now, I *assumed* that the second adult in each room was there to teach but, honestly, none of those second teachers were actually teaching children. So by my count, that's four teachers that, in a way, you've lost."

The principal looked at me as my observation sunk in, until the bell rang and the cafeteria was flooded with students clamoring for food like a pack of rabid wolves. Later that day, we met up again, and the principal ushered me into her office.

"You were right," she told me. "I have lost *at least* four teachers! I wonder if this is happening in other classrooms? I need every one of my teachers *teaching*. I didn't even see this problem, and it is right in front of me!"

Whether it's with respect to our watch face, or our workplace, or our relationships, leaders need to understand the following principle:

We see what we expect to see.

Leaders Lead Self-Examined Lives

Though that principal certainly held a position of leadership within her school (and was quite good at her job, I might add), the morning we spent together shows how easy it is to let certain aspects of our jobs, our relationships, and our lives go blissfully unexamined. We may have two perfectly healthy eyes, but are we *really* seeing what is right in front of us? Or are we letting our preconceived notions, filters of our own experiences, and faulty assumptions cloud our perspective? If we're not careful, it's all too easy to fall into the latter.

Good leaders, by contrast, lead self-examined lives. And as a result, they have a highly developed sense of self-awareness – one of the least discussed leadership qualities, but one of the most valuable. Self-awareness is all about being conscious of what you're good at and where your skills and strengths lie, while acknowledging your weaknesses and areas in which you still have plenty yet to learn. To achieve that level of self-awareness, you have to look into what I call blind spots, which we'll talk more about in Chapter 7. Looking into our blind spots can be a painful process, and one that encompasses the touchy work of admitting when you – not your spouse, your boss, or even your circumstances – are to blame for the problem.

We may have two perfectly healthy eyes, but are we really seeing what is right in front of us?

Alignment: Not Just For Tires

Tires aren't the only things that can get out of alignment. If we Examine Everything, we can see that misalignment happens all the time with people, organizations, expectations, and relationships, too.

From small nonprofits to large corporations, it's all the rage these days to determine and develop an organization's mission, values, and vision. Corporations spend lots of time (and usually money) identifying these philosophies and principles, as well as fine-tuning and tweaking them. But all too often they exist only on paper, in new employee handbooks that are read once and then gather dust on the far end of a cubicle shelf. And all too often there's a total disconnect when it comes to living out those well-crafted words.

Here's what I mean: If an outside party reads your company or organization's mission statement and then spends time observing your behavior and the behavior of your organization or team, will they see congruence? Will the behaviors, attitudes, reactions, and responses align with what you *say* is important to you or your organization?

Furthermore, is how you live your life – how you spend your time, how you act toward others, how you represent yourself, whether you're running errands or posting on Facebook or having lunch in the break room – in alignment with your values as an employee, or a parent, or a friend?

For the woman in the following story, which is an edited version of an anecdote that ended up in my inbox not too long ago, I'd say the answer is definitely no.

> *The light turned yellow, just in front of the driver. He did the right thing, stopping at the crosswalk, even though he could have accelerated through the intersection and beaten the light.*

> *The driver just a few feet behind his car honked her horn in fury, screaming in frustration, as she, too, was stuck at the light.*

> *Still in mid-rant, she heard a tap on her window and looked up into the face of a somber police officer. He ordered her to exit her car with her hands up.*

> *He took the woman to the police station where she was searched, fingerprinted, photographed, and placed in a holding cell. Her road rage was now replaced by fury over why she was being held in custody, but nobody gave her any answers, and she was too scared to press for a reason.*

After a while, a policeman approached the cell, opened the door, and escorted the woman back to the booking desk, where the arresting officer was waiting with her personal effects.

The officer said, "I'm very sorry for this mistake. You see, I pulled up behind your car while you were blowing your horn and going ballistic at the guy in front of you. Then I noticed the 'What Would Jesus Do' and 'Follow Me to Sunday School' bumper stickers, and your chrome-plated Christian fish, so naturally, I assumed you had stolen the car."

Now, who knows whether this really happened, but one thing is for sure: Not only was this woman personally misaligned, she was also misrepresenting her church. So use this powerful little anecdote as a reminder to examine your behaviors and reactions. Are they aligned with what you *say* you value? To your customers? To your team members? To your students? To your spouse? To your neighbors? To your kids?

If you're out of alignment – and it happens to all of us at some points in our lives – then put some attention and effort to getting realigned. Leaders are adept at this: Examining Everything, starting with their own behavior, so they can develop as accurate a picture of reality, of what's really going on, as possible.

Leaders have the ability to be broadly focused and yet minutely focused, depending on the situation.

Leaders are constantly taking stock of the people, relationships, dynamics, workplaces, and situations around them. At times, a leader needs to be able to examine the big picture; in other words, they need to look at something with some distance, like an astronomer uses a telescope. Other times, they focus their attention on something, like a scientist examines with microscope. Leaders have the ability to be broadly focused and yet minutely focused, depending on the situation. Either way, leaders are continually observing and examining.

Examining Everything requires a conscious choice to tune into our surroundings, whether they take the form of people's behaviors, specific situations, office dynamics, or any number of infinite other possibilities that make up this crazy train called life. As a colleague of mine says, we need to be "in the moment, at the moment."

And that awareness means tapping into more than our sense of sight.

Can You Hear Me Now?

"Can you hear me now?" The catchphrase of the upbeat Verizon Wireless guy, walking across the country and around the world making sure the Verizon network is operating at optimum efficiency. Over and over he asks, "Can you hear me now?" to the person on the other end of the phone. The phrase earned its 15 minutes of fame in our pop culture vernacular, much to the delight of Verizon, I'm sure.

Technology issues notwithstanding, the task of the Verizon guy is fairly simple: All he needs to know is whether the person on the other end of the phone can physically hear him. Whether they're listening, however, is another question entirely.

This powerful subtlety – the difference between hearing someone and *really* listening – is a skill that leaders are adept at. Hearing is, if you're blessed with good health, the easy part; it's the listening that trips us up. But listening is a critical aspect of Examining Everything. It's another way of observing and taking in the world around us.

Just as importantly: To listen well, as an old Chinese proverb goes, is as powerful a means of influence as to talk well.

Hearing is the easy part; it's the listening that trips us up.

A few years ago, I was conducting a leadership workshop for a group of executives, a close-knit bunch who worked for the same organization. As part of the program, I gave them what I refer to as an Effective Listening Test. To their collective shock, only one of the executives passed – and he was wearing a hearing aid! He teased the others, saying, "Oh man, are we in trouble – the only one who was really listening was the deaf guy!" We all had a good laugh, but the point was well made.

When the others asked how they could have done so poorly, I confessed that I had created a slight distraction by jingling coins, something that could have made it a bit harder for them to concentrate on the test. When they asked why I would "sabotage" them and their results, I explained how the test was representative of all the real-life distractions they face in running their organization. In fact, my jingling of the coins was minimal compared to the issues they were dealing with in the day-to-day operation of their organization. Only the executive who had honed his concentration and observation skills, due to his hearing impediment, was able to accurately interpret what I was saying.

Are *You* Really Listening?

True story: A preacher was in Indianapolis to speak at a conference. While staying at a prominent hotel across the street, he was waiting in the lobby for a colleague. They planned to have breakfast, and as he was browsing the newspaper while he waited, a well-dressed woman approached him and asked if he was one of the preachers speaking at the conference across the street.

He said that he was, and she asked if she might have a word with him.

He answered that she could, and, concerned for the woman's privacy, the preacher escorted her over to a quiet corner of the lobby where he could still keep an eye out for his friend.

The woman introduced herself and explained what she did: that she was a prostitute who frequented this hotel with her clients. Before the preacher could even respond, she shared a fascinating detail about her profession: "Half the men who pay for my body never touch me. They just want someone to talk to, and I'm a very good listener."

As the preacher stood there, stunned, the woman went on to explain that if he would share this story with his congregation, there might be a marriage or two that could be vastly improved – or even saved. The preacher did share her message that very morning at the conference, where my parents, who were in attendance, heard it and then later told me.

We may be hearing a lot of words coming out of their mouths, but are we really listening?

I share this story with you now not to blame wives for their cheating husbands (or to suggest that this prostitute was acting as a leader), but to offer a stark example of the power of just listening to others.

Take a minute to consider whether you're really listening:
- to your team members?
- to your kids?

- to your spouse?
- to your co-workers?
- to your friends?
- to your students?

We may be *hearing* a lot of words coming out of their mouths, but are we really *listening?* You see, many times the message is not in the words, the "what"; it's in the how: how those words are delivered, the body language they're delivered with, or what isn't being said. Is the project team really working well together – which they appeared to be when you stuck your head into the meeting – or are some of the members not fully disclosing thoughts and concerns because it is not a safe environment to be totally honest? Is your spouse, child, or colleague just being quiet, or is their silence an indication that something is bothering them?

Just like we see what we expect to see:

We hear what we expect to hear.

But listening well helps cuts through that blockage. Leaders have the ability to really listen, observe, and tune in to all the cues around them. In other words, leaders don't get lazy with their senses, or take the easy way out when someone is saying one thing with their mouth and something entirely different with their body language. While people have to be responsible for speaking their own truth, a leader has a knack for working well with people who have trouble communicating what they

Leaders don't get lazy with their senses.

really mean. They ask hard-hitting questions and aren't afraid of the answers.

This is one more component of what it means to Examine Everything. And it's a critical life and leadership skill, because we can become so busy and so preoccupied that we don't even notice what is going on right in front of us. The damage from that ignorance can be devastating and shocking: a spouse filing for divorce, a child running away from home, a coworker leaving an organization, a top customer switching to a competitor, or a founding partner wanting out of the business.

In order to prevent such situations from ever reaching that breaking point in the first place, we have to do more than just opening our eyes and ears.

You see, in this age of information overload (phones, e-mails, TV with hundreds of channels, satellite radio, text messages, social media), it's easy – understandable, even – to get lazy with our observation skills. Sure, when our spouse or colleague asks, "Are you listening to me?" we can parrot back everything they just said. But do we really understand what they mean, where they're coming from, what kind of a response they're looking for from us? Or were we focused on our overflowing inbox, the overdue project, the ball game, or which unlucky contestant would be voted off *Dancing With the Stars?* The best we have to give is all of ourselves: to our children, our spouses, our colleagues, our direct reports. If we're not giving them our full attention when the situation demands it, what are we communicating? That these people aren't important enough to us. That they're not worthy of our full attention.

If we're not giving them our full attention, what are we communicating?

Take a quick second to ask yourself if you're giving the person or situation around you the attention they deserve. If you were to stand back and look at the scene unfolding, do you want to be the kind of father who's immersed in college football every weekend and ignoring his child? Do you want to be the kind of manager who checks e-mail or sends text messages while she is giving an annual review? Do you want to be the kind of friend who meets a girlfriend who's having a rough day for a cup of coffee, only to vent about your own problems instead of giving your full attention to her?

A Heartbreaking Letter And A Lesson On Listening

If nothing else sinks in from this chapter, I hope the message from the following letter does. It's from a boy in prison, sent to his parents, who then sent it on to hopefully help other parents avoid making the same mistakes they did. I don't remember who I received it from years ago, but its impact has stayed with me ever since.

As you'll read, these poor parents failed to Examine Everything in their family dynamics: They weren't around enough to listen to their son when he was growing up and they missed cues from him desperately pleading for their attention. In short, by the time they did clue in to his situation, it was too late.

> *"It is too late for us, because the damage has been done, but maybe if we share his letter it will help other parents. Thank you very, very much."*
> — *Parents of the letter writer*

Dear Folks,

Thank you for everything, but I am going to Chicago and try to start some kind of new life.

You asked me why I did those things and why I gave you so much trouble, and the answer is easy for me to give you, but I am wondering if you will understand.

*Remember when I was about six or seven and I used to want you to **just listen to me?** I remember all the nice things you gave me for Christmas and my birthday and I was real happy with the things for about a week but the rest of the year I really didn't want presents. **I just wanted all the time for you to listen to me like I was somebody** who felt things too, because I remember even when I was young I felt things. But you said you were too busy.*

Mom, you are a wonderful cook, and you had everything so clean and you were so tired so much from doing all those things that made you busy, but you know something, Mom? I would have liked crackers and peanut butter just as well – if you had only sat down with me a little while during the day and said to me: "Tell me all about it so I can maybe help you understand."

If [my sister] ever has children, I hope you will tell her to just pay some attention to the one that doesn't smile very much, because that one will be really crying inside. And when she's about to bake six dozen cookies, to make sure first that the kids don't want to tell her about a dream or a hope or something, because thoughts are important too, to small kids even though they don't have so many words to use when they tell about what they have inside them.

*I think all the kids who are doing so many things that the grownups are tearing their hair out or worry about are really looking for somebody that will have the time **to listen a few minutes** and who really and truly will treat them as they would a grownup who might be useful to them. If you folks had ever said to me: 'Pardon me' when you interrupted me, I'd have dropped dead. If anybody asks you where I am, tell them I have gone looking for somebody with time, because I've got a lot of things I want to talk about.*

Love to all,
Your son

This painful letter (Author's note: Words bolded for emphasis, and original letter shortened in this book), also illustrates another critical concept in Leadership Redefined, which I call Exchanging Non-Essentials. We'll look at it in the next chapter.

But before we go there, it's critical to understand one final concept about Examining Everything: It's such a crucial skill for leaders because, as we've all heard, *knowledge is power*. If the parents in the above letter, for example, had Examined Everything with respect to raising their son, it's a pretty safe bet they would have been aware of his need for more attention from them – and they could have changed their behavior for the better, and possibly prevented his troubled path in life, as well as avoided such a heartbreaking rift in their relationship. If Ron, the bold fellow who bet me about his watch, had done a better job noticing the details of that timepiece (a cherished gift from his father, remember!), I highly doubt he would have ever put himself in such a powerless position in front of the entire audience.

Take the time to stop, look, and really listen in your life. Examine Everything, and watch your positive influence grow exponentially.

EXPLORE ON YOUR OWN

1. Think of a time when you saw or experienced something and thought you "knew" exactly what happened, only to realize you were completely wrong or did not have the whole picture. Describe what happened.

2. What do the phrases "We see what we want to see" and "We hear what we want to hear" mean to you?

3. Think about a time when you inadvertently may have allowed preconceived ideas, notions, filters, or perspectives to cause you to not really see what was right in front of you.

4. Describe an incident when you encountered someone whose words and/or actions did not align with what they or their organization said they believed or stood for. How did it make you feel?

5. Describe a time when you were trying to speak to someone and they clearly were not listening to you. How did it make you feel?

6. Is it possible that we do the same thing to others? How could this impact our relationship with them? How could this impact our success or lack thereof?

7. When you get out of alignment, how can you get back on track (Hint: Chapter 2)?

8. Identify someone you could ask to hold you accountable for telling you when you are misaligned in your behavior or attitude. When will you ask for their input?

9. How can using the stop, look, and listen strategy help you Examine Everything in your life?

10. In this chapter, there's a list of different people in your life. Here they are again. Rank how well you believe you listen to them from 1-5 (with 1 being "I don't listen to them at all" to 5 being "I am fully listening"). Then ask them how they think you're doing, and record their ranking as well.

People	Your Rank	Their Rank
Team Members	____	____
Kids	____	____
Spouse	____	____
Co-workers	____	____
Friends	____	____
Students	____	____
Relatives	____	____

CHAPTER 4
EXCHANGE
NON-ESSENTIALS

Don't be afraid to give up the good to go for the great.
  - John D. Rockefeller

It was nearly 8 a.m. on a cold January morning in 2007. A street musician had just set up a makeshift performance venue in a Washington, D.C. subway station near some escalators and a trash can. Dressed in jeans, a long-sleeved T-shirt, and a Washington Nationals baseball cap, the musician, a youngish Caucasian male, opened his case and dropped in a few bucks to inspire others to open their wallets. Then, amidst the morning rush hour bustle, he began playing his violin.

Over the next 43 minutes, the musician played six songs. Exactly 1,097 people would walk past him, but only seven stopped to take in the performance for a moment or two. Twenty-seven people gave money, for a grand total of $32.17, but most of them never even broke stride.

That leaves well more than 1,000 people who hurried by, oblivious. Many didn't even bother to glance at the musician; neither did dozens of customers who lined up to buy lottery tickets at a nearby kiosk.

You know what all these people missed? A live performance by none other than Joshua Bell, one of the world's preeminent violinists. Just days earlier, Bell had played to a standing-room-only crowd where average seats cost about $100 apiece. The six songs he played in the subway station that January morning were some of the most beautiful, complex masterpieces ever written. Bell played them on a violin sometimes referred to as a "Strad," which had been handcrafted by world-renowned violinist Antonio Stradivari himself in 1713. The instrument itself is worth well over $3.5 million.

The Washington Post had arranged this performance as a social experiment, and it is amazing – and disheartening, especially if you watch the video of it – to see hundreds of people rushing past with nary a glance at Bell. As I reflect on the story, I realize that I, too, probably would have raced on by and missed one of the best violinists in the world, playing the best music in the world on the best violin in the world. Do you think you would have, too?

If we're too busy to stop for just a few minutes to take in some beautiful music, what else are we missing in our lives?

Why?

It goes beyond simply not recognizing the incognito Joshua Bell – very few people could have, unless they were classical music fans. More important to consider is this: If we're too busy to stop for just a few minutes to take in some beautiful music, played by one of the world's most superb musicians, what else are we missing in our lives?

And how can we make room for the most important stuff?

It starts with learning how to Exchange Non-Essentials.

Our Increasingly Busy Lives

For nearly 25 years, one of the most frequently requested training programs I have conducted is an advanced time management and personal organization workshop titled *"I'm Spread*

So Thin You Can See Through Me." In this course I teach people how they can learn to manage every detail of their life and never have anything fall through the cracks.

Thousands of people have participated in the program, and I often ask attendees why they sign up and come. Ninety-nine percent of the time, they say the title drew them in and prompted them to register.

Can you identify with it? Most people can. These days, there are more demands on our time and attention than ever before. We live in a society that's truly 24-7-365, thanks to new communications technology like Facebook, Twitter, and Skype (and who knows what else will be added to the mix by the time you read this book); increased pressure for productivity; aging parents; a still-sluggish economy; and to-do lists that never seem to end.

These days, there are more demands on our time and attention than ever before.

The stats and figures documenting our Mach-speed existences are staggering: One research firm estimated that in 2010 the *number of e-mails* sent *per day* was around 294 billion. Another company, Nielsen, puts the number of texts that just one teenager sends at 3,000 per month. And not only is the volume of our communication and contact greater, but everything seems to be the most important thing.

Does this describe your life? (Or are you too busy to answer?)

It's no surprise, then, that stress levels in our society are at an all-time high. Not all stress is inherently bad, however. Acute stress, which is also known as the fight-or-flight response, is how your body reacts immediately to a threat, danger, scare, or challenge, whether it's real or perceived. The acute-stress response is immediate and intense, and depending on the person and the situation, it can be thrilling (such as zooming through the treetops on a zipline), lifesaving (warding off an attacker), or addictive (skydivers who need an adrenaline fix). Acute stress doesn't generally cause health problems for most people, and it can actually be helpful by driving you to act and motivating you toward your goals.

Stress levels in our society are at an all-time high.

Chronic stress, however, is another story. Chronic stress happens when those acute stressors – bills, medical issues, caring for a sick or elderly relative, teenagers in general – pile up and stick around. Chronic stress feels much more overwhelming and disheartening than acute stress, and its effects can be much more severe. These stress-influenced conditions include anxiety, depression, diabetes, ulcers, obesity, heart disease, hyperthyroidism, tight muscles, and a whole host of other health problems.

Chronic stress is sometimes compared to holding a glass of water with your arm outstretched for a long period of time. Try holding that glass of water for a minute. No big deal, right? But hold it for an hour, and your arm will really start to ache. And if you try to hold it for a day? Impossible – your body simply can't withstand the burden.

It's the same thing with chronic stress. If we carry our stresses all the time without a way to release them and recharge, sooner or later, we'll be crushed under their weight. Just like with the glass of water, we need to be able to put them down for a while before trying to hold them again.

But when you look at the stats on stress and burnout, it seems that, collectively, we're not doing that. More now than ever, people are teetering on a ragged edge. According to a study by the American Psychological Association, more than 43 percent of American adults suffer negatively from stress. And, according to the American Stress Institute, more than 70 percent of visits to the doctor are caused by stress. Stress rears its ugly head in varying but persistent ways: road rage, marital tension, loss of enjoyment in activities you once enjoyed. Just take a look at the hunched-shouldered, zoned-out masses shuffling through a subway station during rush hour, and indeed, it seems like we're all walking zombies just trying to make it through the day.

It seems like we're all walking zombies just trying to make it through the day.

Some relief from all this stress via sleep would be great – if we could get to sleep in the first place. Research on sleep, or rather the lack of it, is astounding: More than 70 million Americans are afflicted by the lack of sleep or some type of sleeping disorder. It's clearly an equal opportunity condition, affecting people at virtually every stage of life. Sixty-four percent of teens blame it for poor school performance, and the most severe cases of sleep deprivation occur between the ages of 30 and 40. Even the elderly are impacted: According to one study, 50 percent of the 65-and-over crowd are affected.

Coping Strategies For Stress

Now that you're probably even more stressed reading about how stressed you are and how stressful life can be, onto some possible solutions! First of all, it's important to realize that no matter what we do, there's no way to completely eliminate stress from our lives. But there are useful coping mechanisms. No doubt you're familiar with some of them:

- Exercise
- Meditation
- Laughter
- A strong network of friends
- Maintaining good nutrition
- Participating in hobbies you enjoy

Research indicates there are many more useful strategies, but one I believe we need to add to the list is what I call Exchanging Non-Essentials. It's related to a principle I learned from author Jim Collins in his bestseller *Good to Great: Why Some Companies Make the Leap ... and Others Don't:*

Don't let the good things rob you of the best things.

There are many good things that can compete for our time, energy, attention, and resources: special projects at work, church committees, environmental efforts, social causes, fantasy sports teams, even enjoying our favorite television shows – the list goes on and on. But if these good things are consistently interfering with doing the *best* things in your life (and only you can determine what those priorities are), then your life will certainly start to feel out of balance after a while. You'll feel the stress of not being able to do it all, as well as a niggling sense of frustration and dissatisfaction. For you, the best things might be spending time with your family and friends, cultivating your health and well-being, traveling, or advancing your career – or a combination of all those. For many people, these are the essentials to leading a fulfilling, successful life. They're what fill up the happiness bucket.

If you're not able to do those best things, then you need to start taking a harder look at the good things – in other words, all the things that *are not* the best things – and how you can limit them. It's the good things that sneak into our lives, taking up the most time and energy and preventing us from focusing on the best. Take a minute and ask yourself: Could you do a better job of letting some of those good things in your life go, so that you have more time to enjoy and appreciate the best things?

If the answer is yes, then it's time to start Exchanging Non-Essentials.

That's What I've Been Looking For

Sometimes, Exchanging Non-Essentials can come in the form of a simple shift in mindset. In his book *Money: A User's Manual,* finance guru Bob Russell uses an anecdote with a compelling lesson: that it's easy to look past what we already have. Russell tells the story of a farmer who once grew discontented with his farm. The farmer griped about the lake on his property that always needed to be stocked and managed. He complained about all those stupid cows wandering around his land. He lamented the fencing, feeding and upkeep, maintenance – the list went on and on. This farm was turning out to be nothing but a headache, the farmer began to think.

Could you do a better job of letting some of those good things in your life go?

So one day the farmer called a real estate agent and made plans to put his farm up for sale. A few days later the agent phoned the farmer to get approval for the advertisement she would place in the local paper. She read the ad to the farmer. It described a lovely farm in an ideal location: quiet and peaceful, contoured with rolling hills, carpeted with soft meadows, nourished by a fresh lake, and blessed with well-bred livestock.

The farmer said, "Read that ad to me again."

So the real estate agent did. And after hearing it a second time, the farmer thought to himself: "I've changed my mind. I'm not going to sell my farm. I've been looking for a place like it all my life."

Aren't we like that farmer? I know I am. Sometimes I get so caught up in the daily grind of life that I lose sight of what really matters – and all the great things I already have around me.

That's part of the context of Exchanging Non-Essentials: learning to purge, and getting rid of those things in our lives that are distracting us from appreciating and nurturing the most important things in our lives, whether they're family, friends, our health, spirituality. Or a beloved farm. Or stopping for a moment to enjoy world-class music.

The Main Thing

Here's another way to describe the objective of Exchanging Non-Essentials:

> ***The main thing***
> ***is to keep the main thing***
> ***the main thing.***

Take a moment to inventory all the things you are busy doing and being. Are they all necessary, or could you pare down some of them to free up the time you need to focus on what really matters in your life – the main thing?

An easy, quick way to test this is to look at your calendar for the past year. How did you spend your time? Then, compare your schedule with your most important priorities for your life. Do they align? No? Time to Exchange Non-Essentials.

Put Right Things First

Instead of putting first things first, Exchanging Non-Essentials is about putting right things first. And that means focusing on the right target, which can be easier said than done.

Consider the story of U.S. Olympic rifle shooter Matthew Emmons. On August 13, 2004, Emmons won a gold medal in rifle shooting in the Summer Games in Athens, Greece. He was gunning for his second gold medal that year, in the 50-meter three-position rifle event, and the New Jersey shooter was hoping to bury the field with a bull's-eye on his final shot.

Take a moment to inventory all the things you are busy doing. Are they all necessary?

Emmons' turn arrived, and he aimed, exhaled, and squeezed his shot off. But Emmons' score didn't register. That's because he *hit the wrong target*. In an extremely rare mistake at that level of elite competition, Emmons had cross-fired. His focus had been on the wrong spot – a bull's-eye on the target in the next lane. That error cost Emmons the gold medal, dropping him to eighth place.

Emmons' mistake was one of the most disheartening stories of the Games that year. And although they haven't necessarily been misses on an Olympic level, we've all missed the target at some point in our lives – because we've been focused on the wrong thing.

Leaders, however, realize the importance of focusing on the correct targets, whatever those may be in their lives. They make progress on purpose, in their professions, their relationships, their personal self-growth, because they have fine-tuned their ability to focus on the right things.

But in order to focus on the right target, you have to figure out what that target is (which, as you may remember, is all about Extracting a Goal), and how it's related to your value system on a bigger scale. For example, Exchanging Non-Essentials may come with a re-evaluation of your priorities, or re-examining traditional notions of success, and what that means to you.

The Jamaican Fisherman

I once heard a powerful anecdote that hammers home this message. It centers on a Jamaican fisherman, an American businessman, and the notion of success. It goes something like this: The American businessman was on vacation in a small Jamaican fishing village when a small boat manned by a solo local fisherman docked on a nearby pier.

The fisherman began to haul out his catch: several large tuna, which the American complimented. He asked the fisherman how long it took to catch them.

"Jus' a little while," the fisherman replied. The American then asked why he didn't stay out longer and catch more fish, to which the Jamaican said he had caught enough to support his family's immediate needs.

The American then asked how the Jamaican spent the rest of his time. The fisherman said, "Sleep late, fish, play wid me pickney [the word Jamaicans use for children], mek love wid me wife, tek a stroll inna de village each evening where me drink rum and play domino wid me bredren [friends]. Me have a full and busy life, mon!"

The American replied: "I have my MBA from *[insert your favorite High-Falutin' Big-Time Business School]*. Let me just suggest a few ideas to help you. You should spend more time fishing and with the money you make, you can buy a bigger boat. Then, with a bigger boat, you can catch more fish, make more money, and buy several boats. Eventually you would have a fleet of fishing boats, and instead of selling your catch to a middleman, you could sell directly to the processor, eventually opening your own cannery!"

The businessman's eyes grew wide, and he rubbed his hands together excitedly, continuing: "You would control everything: the product, processing, and distribution. You would need to leave this village and move to Kingston, then maybe Los Angeles, and then probably New York City, where you would run your growing fishing empire!"

The Jamaican fisherman asked, "But mon, how long will all dis tek?"

The businessman replied, "Probably about 15 to 20 years, give or take."

"Den wha' me a' do next, mon?"

The businessman laughed, smiled, and said, "That's the best part! When the time is right you would announce an IPO and sell your company stock to the public and cash in. You could make millions!"

"Millions, mon? Den wha'?" asked the Jamaican, with a quiet smile on his lips.

This made the American pause. He then humbly answered, "Then you would retire and move to a small fishing village, where you would sleep late, fish, play with your kids, make love with your wife, and take walks into the village in the evenings, where you would drink rum and play dominoes with your friends."

Instead of chasing after fame and wealth, the Jamaican fisherman was living a simple, day-to-day existence fishing only for what his family needed to live. He cherished one-on-one time with his children, wife, and friends, walking in his beloved village and indulging in fine Jamaican rum. Instead of working himself to death for 15 to 20 years to finally have "the good life," he was already living it.

In his own way, the Jamaican fisherman had Exchanged Non-Essentials and had created for himself the happiest, most fulfilling existence possible. And, in his own way, he was also acting as a leader, by influencing the businessmen to think about the notion of success in a very different way.

I think we could all take a lesson from him.

Margins: Not Just For Word Documents

Remember Joshua Bell and his violin experiment in the subway station? It illustrates another important component of Exchanging Non-Essentials: the idea of margins.

You see, many people have crammed their days with so many activities and events, tasks and to-do's, schedules and just plain *Margins are where change can take place. Where growth can happen. Where opportunities can arise.* "stuff," that we have no margins in our lives. You see, margins go far beyond a function in Microsoft Word, which we all know is that white space all the way around a document where there is nothing. On a page, margins give our eyes a chance to rest. They frame the important stuff, of course, but they play another important role, too: Think about how difficult it is to read and comprehend words and paragraphs on a page that extend all the way to the edge, with no space or buffer. Without margins, the content would be overwhelming.

Creating margins for our lives is equally important. Most people fill their days completely up, from morning to night, week to week, month to month, year to year. But by Exchanging Non-Essentials – minimizing or removing the unnecessary time-sucks, activities, or responsibilities that don't move us toward our goals, enhance our lives, or align with our values – we not only free up critical time, space, and energy for the most important things in our lives, but we also create margins.

Margins are where change can take place. Where growth can happen. Where opportunities can arise, often cloaked as inconveniences or interruptions.

For example, margins allow you to be fully available when your colleague walks into your office, closes the door, and tells you that he and his spouse are divorcing. Margins enable you to drop everything when your son comes home from school and wants to talk about something that happened that's bugging him. Margins allow you to help a neighbor whose cat has run away.

I learned a great lesson about Exchanging Non-Essentials from Doris, my mother-in-law. I remember one Saturday afternoon when she was visiting us *(ok, let's not fool ourselves: She was there to see her two grandkids. My wife and I just happened to live in the same house as they did)*. Tina, my bride, was lamenting about being so busy and so tired and how frustrated and embarrassed she was that the house was a mess and she hadn't had time to vacuum or dust or anything else.

"Leave that dust alone, honey, and go read a book to those babies, because in a blink you will have nothing but dust."

Doris, herself a mother of five, looked straight into Tina's eyes and said something I will never forget: "Leave that dust alone, honey, and go read a book to those babies, because in a blink you will have nothing *but* dust."

Exchanging Non-Essentials to build margins is what allows a leader to see what normally might be perceived as an interruption or an inconvenience and turn it into an opportunity. An opportunity to influence. An opportunity to help someone else. An opportunity appreciate the beauty and blessings of one's own life – like a bucolic farm, or having enough fish to feed your family, or the simple joy of listening to beautiful music in the subway on your way to work.

A Key Question

So how do we Exchange Non-Essentials? It's a never-ending quest, as your life changes and your priorities shift. But no matter where you are in life, there's a very simple question you can ask yourself that may reveal some profound insight about how you're spending your valuable time:

Why are you doing what you're doing?

The question applies to all areas of your life, from something as broad as your career to something as seemingly mundane as playing another game of Angry Birds. Are you doing it because it's what everyone else is doing? Are you doing it out of obligation? Habit? Responsibility? Necessity? Boredom? Fear? Because you got sucked in, it's brainless, and it's easier to keep doing it than changing? The concern that, if you don't do it, it won't get done?

To that, I ask, so what? Maybe this effort or project, whatever it is, doesn't need to get done – or at least not by you anymore.

Take, for example, a couple at a Sunday school class I used to teach. For years, this lovely couple volunteered to arrive at church extra early to get the coffee ready. Now, this was a big class, with more than 150 people coming every week, so there was quite a lot coffee to brew.

One Sunday morning before class, the couple nervously approached me. They explained that since now they were parents of young twins, it was just too much to get to church every week for coffee duty. Sunday mornings had gotten quite hectic in their home, and they couldn't swing the responsibility anymore. I thanked them for their years of help and told them not to worry about it. I would simply announce to the class that someone else needed to step up.

That very Sunday I announced the opening and asked any interested folks to see me after class. None did. And as a non-coffee person, I really didn't care.

The following Sunday there was no coffee. There was none the next Sunday either, or the next. And you know what? It was no big deal. The people who *were* coffee drinkers either pilfered some from other classrooms, or they grabbed a cup on their way to church.

In your own life, are you a Coffee Couple (or person), busy doing things that you think are oh-so-important, that you believe others really need *you* to do – when in reality, those things aren't important enough to justify your time?

It's also important to make the distinction that there are situations where we'd certainly rather be doing something else – sipping a mai tai on the beach instead of punching the clock at the factory, for example. In other words, you may not consider your job one of the best things in your life. However, it's *Are you busy doing things that you think are oh-so-important?* a necessary means to be able to enjoy the best things in your life, such as supporting your family, for example, or enabling you to travel.

Lessons From The Coffee Couple

The (former) Coffee Couple, as I'll call them, learned to Exchange at least one of the Non-Essentials in their new-to-parenting life with the arrival of their twins. But it doesn't take a major milestone event like that to start seeing the benefits of Exchanging Non-Essentials. Here are a few easy ways you can start doing it – and making room for the right things in your life:

Make no a part of your vocabulary. We all need to take a lesson from the Coffee Couple and learn to start saying no to obligations, responsibilities, or activities that don't enhance our lives, move us toward our goals, or align with the values we deem important.

Limit time watching television and being online. The average U.S. household now contains more televisions than people, and we're watching more television than ever: about three to five hours a day, per person. Another recent report found that Americans spent 53.5 billion total minutes on Facebook in one month – that's roughly 101,720 years. Yes, television and social media play an important role in our digital lives, and they're here to stay. But you can never get back that hour you spent watching kitten videos or some celebrity train wreck throw a fit. So let's make a pledge to put the remotes and mice down for a while, shall we?

Take a hard look at what you value in life and how you spend your time. Do they align?

Identify which are the good things in your life and which are the best things. Make sure you're not spending so much time and energy on the good things that you have nothing left over for the best things.

A Graduation Speech To Remember

Apple co-founder Steve Jobs was no doubt one of history's most brilliant visionaries. The creative genius of Jobs, who died on Oct. 5, 2011 at age 56 after battling pancreatic cancer, forever changed the way we communicate and look at the world around us.

If today were the last day of my life, would I want to do what I am about to do?

In 2005, about a year after he found out he had cancer, Jobs gave a graduation speech to Stanford University. Here's what he said:

> *Remembering that I'll be dead soon is the most important tool that I've ever encountered to help me make the big choices in life. Because almost everything – all external expectations all pride, all fear of embarrassment or failure – these things just fall away in the face of death, leaving only what is truly important. Remembering that you are going to die is the best way I know to avoid the trap of thinking you have something to lose. You are already naked. There is no reason not to follow your heart.*

Pretty serious stuff, especially considering that the audience was a group of eager young college graduates. But Jobs also offered some advice.

> *For the past 33 years I have looked in the mirror every morning and asked myself: "If today were the last day of my life, would I want to do what I am about to do today?" And whenever the answer has been "No" too many days in a row, I know I need to change something.*

Or perhaps *exchange* something – like the Non-Essentials. Start today by turning off the television, logging off the internet, and plugging into what really nourishes you.

EXPLORE ON YOUR OWN

1. What are your major stressors on the job and at home?

2. Who could you ask, "What do you think stresses me most?" When will you ask them?

3. What are the "best" things in life for you?

4. Inventory all the things you are busy doing and being. Are they all necessary?

5. What are the "good" things in your life that might be robbing you from enjoying the "best" things? If you let go of some of those good things, how would it affect your stress?

6. Can you think about how to reduce those good things in your life? How? When will you do this?

7. Compare your activities to what you say you value the most. How can you achieve more alignment between them?

8. Identify something in your life that you need to say no to.

9. For many, television and the internet have become major time thieves. What are some things you could do instead of spending time on these? Would that lower your stress? Would that increase your enjoyment of the "best things"? Why?

CHAPTER 5
EXPECT OPPOSITION

Great minds have always encountered violent
opposition from mediocre minds.
- Albert Einstein

It was Sir Isaac Newton who discovered that for every action, there's an equal and opposite reaction. Indeed, Newton's theory, which is called his Third Law of Motion, was a game-changer for the world of physics.

But it also can apply in a less literal context: interpersonal relationships.

Think about it: How many times have you expressed an idea for something, whether it's a new business, a revitalized way to generate sales, even a different way to handle the volunteer schedule for your kid's soccer team, and been met with something along these lines:

"I'm not sure that will work."
"That's not the way we do it around here."
"Are you crazy? That will never make money."
"We'd better stick with the current system."

So, as a leader, how can you best deal with that kind of opposition? You'll be way ahead of the game if you expect it.

A Constant Element

Along with death and taxes, opposition – or conflict – in whatever form it may take, is a certainty in our lives. Wars throughout all eras of history have happened because of opposing ideas, beliefs, and world powers. Opposition and conflict are critical elements across all strata of human existence, from the sports arena to the courts system to the conference table at the office.

Opposition usually occurs when there are differing thoughts on a proposed action, belief, or idea that may be worth investigating. In addition, conflict may naturally arise when people with diverse backgrounds come together in a group setting. In this respect, conflict and opposition can help strengthen the final results. They can hone an idea. They can expose weaknesses and areas that need fine-tuning.

Along with death and taxes, opposition, or conflict, in whatever form it may take, is a certainty in our lives.

When you boil it down, without opposition and conflict, life would be kind of, well, boring. *(And millions of lawyers would be out of jobs.)*

That said, too much opposition can be dangerous. It has the potential to destroy dreams, stifle innovation, and suppress growth, both on individual and global levels. Consider the following:

When the Decca Recording Company rejected the Beatles in 1962, the company said it didn't like the young British group's sound, claiming that guitar music was on the way out of mainstream popularity.

The founder of Warner Brothers, H.M. Warner, wanted to know "Who the hell wants to hear actors talk?" before he rejected a proposal for "talkies," or movies made with sound in the mid-1920s.

When Debbi Fields went to a potential investor for her idea of a cookie store, she was told that it was "a bad idea" and that market research indicated that "America likes crispy cookies, not soft and chewy cookies like you make." Fields went on to found Mrs. Fields' Cookies *(and probably added to America's obesity epidemic in the process. But I digress.)*

A Yale professor similarly labeled Fred Smith's paper proposing the idea of reliable overnight delivery service "unfeasible." Smith went on to found Federal Express Corporation, known these days as FedEx.

It's no secret that every one of the people behind those "bad" or unfeasible ideas created something that has become a household name. Right from the start, they experienced opposition, but they didn't let it stop them from persevering and taking their idea from dream to reality.

In other words, while I'm sure those individuals were most certainly disappointed by the response they got, they didn't view it as the end of their quest for success or the death of their idea.

Opposition From Within

As with those famous rejections, while opposition often comes from outside sources, it also can be fueled from within, most often by the f-word: FEAR. While this word often conjures up images like knock-kneed, wannabe daredevils too scared to make that step out of the airplane, the emotion also bubbles up in less adrenaline-fueled contexts. For example, many of us have a general fear of failing at something: our jobs, raising our children well, or the ability to successfully change careers.

Leaders are no different. Like everyone else, they experience fear from within. The difference is, they don't let it debilitate them from taking action.

They also seem to understand, at least at a subconscious level, some basic truths about fear:

1. The only way to get rid of the fear of doing something is to go out and do it.

2. Like opposition, fear is a constant in our lives that will never go away as long as you continue to grow.

3. You are not the only person who experiences fear in unfamiliar territory. It happens to everybody.

4. Pushing through fear is much less frightening than living with the underlying frustration and "what if?" that comes from doing nothing.

5. In order to get something you've never had, you must do something you've never done.

Making Dumb Mistakes

In addition to our inside fears, our outside actions can provide opposition against our progress or moving toward our goals or positively influencing the world around us. In other words, sometimes we can make seriously stupid mistakes.

Leaders don't let fear debilitate them from taking action.

For some pretty amusing ones that relate to the sales industry, I highly recommend Dan Seidman's *Death of 20th Century Selling: 50 Hilarious Sales Blunders and How You Can Profit from Them.* The book includes humorous anecdotes of how various individuals in the sales sector managed to shoot themselves in the foot.

For me, one of the most memorable stories was that of Philippe[5], who was working as a sales rep. He was slogging through the tail end of a ridiculously long day setting up promotional displays in stores. He finally wrapped up his last display just as the store was closing up, and a woman walked in insisting to see the sales manager of the store.

In order to get something you've never had, you must do something you've never done.

Philippe wasn't part of the store staff, of course, but he tried to tell the woman how busy the manager was so that he wouldn't have to go to the trouble of tracking him down. All he wanted to do at this point was go home, but the woman insisted he find the manager so she could speak to him.

So Philippe angrily burst into the office of the manager and told him, "Some big fat old battle-ax just waddled into aisle seven demanding to see you."

That big fat old battle-ax happened to be the manager's mother. Not surprisingly, Philippe lost the account.

I've made similarly embarrassing gaffes throughout my career, including walking right off the back of the stage during a presentation. But one that really sticks in my mind as an example of me being my worst enemy happened a few years ago when I secured a meeting with the vice president of operations at a multinational company that specializes in shipping and delivery.

I'd been trying to get a meeting with this woman for months. When I finally did, I did my homework ahead of time. I read up on the company to get a better understanding of their background and what challenges they probably faced in the current business environment, and as a result of all that prep work I aced the meeting.

Until, when she asked for a proposal for my services, I told her I would happily overnight it to her. *Via her main competitor.*

Needless to say, I didn't make the sale.

I bring these up not to make you paranoid of making mistakes – everybody does – but to make you aware that opposition can come not only from around us, but from within too. However, they're much easier to shake off, and learn from, if we drop the expectations of perfection from ourselves (and, while we're at it, everyone else). That's not to say we shouldn't shoot for the stars; in reality, we may just reach the sky, and that's not too shabby.

In other words, nobody's perfect, not even the most seasoned of leaders. Everybody slips and falls from time to time. Leaders, however, have learned how to *fall forward.* By that, I mean not in the physical sense, but using their mistakes – their falls, in other words – as a way to make progress. After all, what's vastly more important than how you fall is how you get up, dust yourself off, and keep going, better prepared for the bumps in the road the next time around.

Leaders have learned how to fall forward.

Unexpected Sources Of Opposition

Sometimes, the *source* of the opposition is what really throws us off our game. Let's face it: There are certain people who you just expect to be against you, and when they raise their ugly heads, it's easier to write them off. But what about when you face opposition from those you think should be in your corner, on your side, or on your team?

I remember one seminar I was conducting a few years ago for a small school district, which was to be held at the newest building in the county, a pre-K through eighth grade facility. As I typically do, I arrived about an hour ahead of time to get set up. I finished early, and the principal asked me if I would like a tour of the new school before we began the program. It was obvious he was quite proud of it, and I was excited to see it, too.

We set off through the halls, and the principal introduced me to staff members and pointed out all the bells and whistles of the new building. The school buzzed with the excitement and anticipation of the upcoming year.

As we entered the fourth grade area, we were almost bowled over by three teachers on their way into a colleague's classroom, laughing like hyenas on caffeine. We followed, not wanting to miss out on the fun, and watched from the door, trying not to look like we were spying.

The teacher into whose room they had raced looked up from her desk as the trio approached. They began wildly rummaging through the papers in front of her.

"Where is it?" they cried. "Show it to us! We know it's here somewhere!"

"What are you doing?" the other teacher asked, surprised. "What are you looking for?"

"Your class roster – where is it?" one asked.

"Here it is!" another teacher shouted, holding it in the air like a trophy. And with eyes as big as big as saucers, they began to run their fingers down the names of students.

"There it is! Ha ha ha! You got him! You got him!" one of them shouted.

The three teachers began laughing and high-fiving. "Yes!" they whooped. "*We* are going to have a good year this year – good luck to you though!"

And as fast as they had entered the room, the teachers disappeared.

I looked at the teacher sitting at her mess of a desk, and I could tell exactly what was going on inside her head. All her high hopes for a positive, successful year filled with discovery and learning had just come crashing down, thanks to the behavior of her colleagues. In less than a minute, her very own fourth-grade co-workers had pulled the rug right out from under her.

I think the principal was as shocked and saddened by what we witnessed as I was. But this tendency to drag down others is nothing new. People have been getting blindsided by those close to them since time began.

A New Lesson In An Old Story

Remember the Bible story about David and Goliath? Most people can at least vaguely recall how the small shepherd boy, David, takes on the horrible, wicked giant, Goliath, and wins by finding a chink in the monster's armor with a stone from his slingshot. Certainly, that story is brimming with lessons, but one aspect of it that some people don't remember is that David's brother Eliab was a vocal opponent of David's ability to take down the giant.

I can just picture Eliab grabbing David's shoulder from behind, spinning him around, and sticking his finger in his brother's chest, saying: "Who do you think you are, talking about taking on Goliath? Ha! You can't even tend that small flock of sheep Father gave you to look after!"

Mediocrity recognizes greatness. It resents it. And it seeks to pull it down.

David's very own family member was a source of scathing opposition in his life. And, sadly, there are lots of Eliabs in the world, but what David did when confronted with that opposition was profound and powerful. In 1 Samuel 17:30, we read: "David turned away from Eliab to another ... "[6]

If you think about it, that's excellent advice when someone tries to cut down your goal, your idea, your dream – turn away from them, and to another. Write them off. Like water off a duck's back, let their words just fall off you. (We'll talk more about exactly what "turning to another means" in the next chapter, Exclude Negative Thinking and Thinkers and Expose Yourself to Winners.)

Beware The Mediocre In Your Midst

So where is all this opposition coming from?

As Einstein expressed in that opening quote from this chapter ("Great minds have always encountered violent opposition from mediocre minds," with which I wholeheartedly agree), a lot of the pushback comes from people who just don't expect to achieve beyond the ordinary in life. The longer I live, the more I see the negative impact that mediocrity can have in virtually any situation. From a mediocre team member pulling the *Cynical people are sometimes nothing more than mediocrity with a bad attitude.* whole team down, to mediocre customer service, to mediocre parenting, mediocrity is something we must try hard to avoid.

Leaders understand that, in their quest to be and do better in every aspect of their lives, they must beware of the mediocre in their midst. Whatever its form, mediocrity recognizes greatness.

It resents it.

And it seeks to pull it down.

Rather than celebrate or emulate success, progress, or greatness, when people who strive for nothing more than mediocrity in their lives encounter people who are aiming much higher, they want to destroy those efforts, consciously or not. You see, great success and achievement – and people who are aiming for those – make the mediocre feel "less than," and rather than work harder to become better, they would rather you become mediocre, too.

While you're at it, watch out for the cynics too. Cynical people are sometimes nothing more than mediocrity with a bad attitude, which they try to mask by cutting everything else down. You can almost hear them rolling their eyes as they talk. In other words,

Cynicism is cancer of the attitude.

These cynics, dream destroyers, or target trashers come in many forms. They could be the (so-called) athlete who tells his teammates to slow down during pre-season wind sprints, or the tech-fearful teacher who tells her colleagues to stop using so much technology in the classroom, or the sales rep who resents a coworker for staying late. The bottom line is that mediocre people do not want to work harder to get better, and they don't like that you do.

See, when you have a goal, dream, or target and you share it, you open yourself up to a wide range of opposition, including questioning, criticism, and sometimes downright ridicule. This opposition usually comes from people who don't have goals, who are content just coasting along, taking the path of least resistance, staying at the status quo, and criticizing others who are venturing off that path. They are comfortable with mediocrity.

Mediocre people do not want to work harder to get better, and they don't like that you do.

These people like to try to build themselves up not by improving themselves but by pulling you down. Just like those teachers who were rejoicing over the fact that the difficult student ended up in their co-worker's classroom, not theirs. No doubt, they were feeling relief over their good fortune. But instead of supporting their co-worker, perhaps offering suggestions for dealing with the challenge she faced, they rubbed their good fortune in her face.

Modern-Day Strategies

No matter where it comes from – as feedback from colleagues, unfounded inner fears, a department head who has been at the company for decades, or even a critical sibling – opposition isn't impossible to overcome. In fact, it's not only surmountable, but also it can serve as a motivation to success.

Here are a few practical, easy-to-employ strategies.

> **Analyze the source of the opposition.** Do the opinions of the opposition represent the majority, or do they merely represent a small, but highly vocal, minority?

> **What is the opposition saying?** Are there valid points being made? If so, consider the opposition as a tool to fine-tune your idea, identify weaknesses, and increase your chances for success.

> **Know when to ignore the opposition and move on.** Follow David's lead here. He knew he had the experience and the heart to fight the giant – and win – and when his brother didn't express support, he simply tuned him out.

As a redefined leader who is choosing to influence others and to make a positive impact on the world around you, you will definitely open yourself up to some opposition. Expect it. Be prepared for it. And don't let it knock you off course, but rather motivate you to keep going.

After all, if you don't ever encounter pushback, criticism, or doubt, that probably means you're not doing much. So consider it as a wake-up call to spring into action. As Elbert Hubbard, an American writer, artist, and publisher once said, "To avoid criticism, do nothing, say nothing, be nothing." Expect Opposition, and when it comes, know that you're already on your way to achieving a dream.

EXPLORE ON YOUR OWN

1. Name some reasons why opposition can be good.

2. Identify something you want to do or try but haven't because you are afraid. How is fear sabotaging your efforts? Look back to the five truths about fear on page 102 and apply them to your current situation. What insights do you now have?

3. How can you apply the concept of "falling forward" on page 104 to a situation you are currently dealing with?

4. Who are the cynics or critics in your life? Knowing who they are, how can you be better prepared to overcome the opposition they throw at you?

5. Have you ever experienced a situation when someone who you thought would support you actually *opposed* your efforts? How did that make you feel? Did you think their opposition was justified, or were you just coming up against their mediocrity?

6. Is it possible that *you* are a source of opposition to someone else? Who? Why? Be careful that mediocrity has not snuck into your thinking.

7. What are you afraid of? How can you apply the five truths about fear to yours?

8. If you knew you wouldn't fail, what would you do? How would that change your approach to reaching your dream, goal, or target?

CHAPTER 6

EXPOSE YOURSELF TO WINNERS
&
EXCLUDE NEGATIVE THINKING

A pessimist sees the difficulty in every opportunity; an optimist sees the opportunity in every difficulty.
— Winston Churchill

If you're a churchgoer in a Christian denomination, chances are you've sung a hymn written by Frances Jane Crosby (her most famous is "Blessed Assurance."). Born in 1820, Crosby, whose nickname was Fanny, wrote more than 9,000 hymns in her lifetime, so many that she was forced to use pen names so hymnal books wouldn't be overflowing with her real name. Crosby's talent in music was just one aspect of her incredible life, though. By age 23, she was addressing Congress and making friendships with presidents. In fact, she knew all the chief executives of her generation.

Just as amazing as her accomplishments is the fact that Crosby achieved them even though she'd been blind since she was an infant, after a quack doctor's treatment of an eye infection left her without her sight. When she was five, her mother recorded one of her prayers: "Oh Lord, help me learn to run and laugh and climb trees like my friends." Crosby's first poem, which she wrote when she was eight years old, illustrated the remarkably positive attitude with which she would continue to lead her life.

Oh, what a happy soul am I,
Although I cannot see.
I am resolved, that in this world,
Contented I will be.
How many blessings I enjoy
That other people don't.
To weep and sigh because I'm blind,
I cannot and I won't.

It's hard to imagine a more positive attitude in anyone, let alone in a blind 8-year-old. Fanny Crosby is an incredibly inspiring example to illustrate the concept of Excluding Negative Thinking. You see, she had every right to be down. She was blinded by no fault of her own, but instead of growing up to be an angry, bitter, spiteful person, she refused to allow a bad attitude – in other words, negative thinking – to be the driving force in her life.

Indeed, leaders inherently understand this principle. It's evident in how they go about their lives by surrounding themselves with positive people and helping to create an encouraging, supportive environment around themselves (or, put another way, Expose Yourself to Winners). They realize that Exposing Themselves to Winners and winning attitudes, like Fanny Crosby's, is a key to developing a positive attitude within themselves.

Exposing Yourself to Winners and winning attitudes is a key to developing a positive attitude within yourself.

Some folks refer to these kinds of influencers as mentors. Others call them heroes. They can be people we know personally or maybe admire from a distance, but they infuse us with energy to do more, be more, and achieve more. These are the people who inspire us to be our best – or at least better than we are right now.

Bottom line: If you're able to actively work toward eliminating negativity in your life, starting with your own thinking and attitude, good things will ensue, for you and the people around you. Indeed, the power of positive thinking can be life-changing. In this chapter, you'll learn how to avoid, eliminate, and minimize the negative thinking *and thinkers* in your life, replacing them with positive thoughts and positive people.

The Father Of Positive Thinking

Have you ever heard of Norman Vincent Peale? This Ohio-born preacher became one of the most influential clergymen of the 20th century, and even if his name doesn't ring a bell, the title of the most popular of his dozens of books surely will: *The Power of Positive Thinking.* Published in 1952, the book is one of the all-time-bestselling self-help guides out there, with more than 20 million copies sold in 40-plus languages.

Peale was a legendary optimist who, until his death in 1993, glowed with charm and kindness that drew people to him and helped them see the good in the world around them. His sermons at his beloved Marble Collegiate Church in Manhattan were so popular that people used to queue up beforehand, prompting a policeman surveying the crowd during Christmas 1981 to say, "You'd think God was holding His closeout sale."[7]

A well-circulated anecdote about Peale involves a man who phoned him one day, deeply depressed and looking for help. Peale invited the man to his office for a chat, during which the man told him he had nothing to live for anymore.

Peale smiled sympathetically at the distraught man sitting before him. "Let's take a look at your situation," he said, taking out a sheet of paper and drawing a line down the middle of the paper. He told the man on the left side they would list the things he'd lost in his life, and on the right, the things he had remaining.

"We won't need that column on the right," the man said. "There's nothing in my life left to live for."

The man said, "There's nothing in my life left to live for."

So Peale asked the man when his wife left him. "She hasn't left me," the man replied, a bit taken aback. "Somehow, she still loves me."

"Well, that's a good start – 'Wife Not Left,'" Peale wrote in the right-hand column. "Now, tell me, when did your children go to jail?"

"What?" the man asked, surprised. "My children aren't in jail!"

"Great!" Peale replied, making more notes. "Then we've got another addition for things you haven't lost – 'Children Not in Jail.'"

After a few more questions along those lines, the man finally saw Peale's point and even allowed a small smile. He said to Peale: "It's funny how things change when you think of them that way."

A Negative Society

It's safe to say we're living in a world with more than its fair share of bitter, angry, and negative people. Sadly, this type of nasty attitude is so commonplace these days that *Saturday Night Live* made an ongoing skit about it a few years ago, with comedian and actress Rachel Dratch as an excellent Debbie Downer.

But it's not quite so funny in real life. Consider, for example, the growing problem of bullying. In recent years, it's become epidemic in schools and online and is the cause of incredible amounts of angst, suffering, and, sadly, even deaths. And that's not to mention the "trolls": The snarky online and internet commenters who post ridiculously mean responses and critical remarks to even the most innocuous item or story.

And it's not just online, either. Next time you're at a kids' sporting event, scan the sidelines, and I bet it won't take long to see a parent screaming like a banshee at the refs, his or her own kids, or even the opponents. A generation ago, the term "road rage" didn't even exist, and now it, as well as its ugly cousin, aggressive driving, is regarded as serious public health threats and major contributors to traffic accidents and deaths. And don't even get me started on all the random shootings in schools, churches, and other public places that have flared up with terrifying regularity in recent years.

Whatever manifestation the negativity takes, however, the offending figures often feel justified in allowing their inner Eeyore to take over their outlook, attitude, and actions. They'll say, "Oh, I'm just a glass half-empty kind of person." Or, "I'm just being honest – what's wrong with that?" Or they enjoy the feeling of putting other people down or belittling others' suc-

We're living in a world with more than its fair share of bitter, angry, and negative people.

cesses or good fortune. And in a society where it's increasingly commonplace to feel outraged when our tiniest need isn't met, or we feel we've been wronged in some way, it's easy to spout off with a misguided sense of entitlement about our rights or privileges as a customer, employee, or deserving human being.

It's exhausting, really, and the Negative Nellies, trolls, bullies, and Debbie Downers of the world have the powerful ability to sabotage the atmosphere around them. Fortunately, there's an antidote to all this nastiness, and it's found within good leaders.

By avoiding and minimizing the influence of negative thinkers – as well as their own negative thinking – on their own attitudes and behaviors, leaders have the ability to rise above negativity. Leaders understand that such an attitude is contagious. Misery does love company, and if you're around it too often, or let it seep into your own outlook, it can be devastating – to both your mental *and* physical health.

Bad Attitudes, Bad Health

Want serious incentive to adopt a sunnier attitude? Consider that in a 30-year study of 447 people at the Mayo Clinic in Dallas[8], researchers found that optimists had about a 50 percent lower risk of early death than pessimists. The study's conclusion was that "mind and body are linked and attitude has an impact on the final outcome – death."

These findings were supported by another study, this one by Yale[9], that asked 660 elderly people whether they agreed that people become less useful as we age. The study participants who didn't agree – in other words, had more positive attitude about aging – lived an average of 7.5 years longer than participants with more negative attitudes, who did agree that we become less useful as we age.

Need more scientific evidence? A Dutch study[10] examined the attitudes and longevity of 999 people older than 65 and reported a "protective relationship" between optimism and mortality. The people with a positive attitude, quite simply, lived longer. They even had a 77 percent lower risk of heart disease than pessimists.

The people with a positive attitude, quite simply, live longer.

Bottom line: Positive thinking leads to healthier people.

The Mohawked Golfer

A few years ago while I was in Orlando for a conference with my family, I was able to squeeze in a round of golf one afternoon. I joined up with Ed and Steve, as we'll call them, who were playing hooky on the final day of another conference they were attending. We warmed up on the driving range and headed to the first tee, the sun bright and warm in the Florida sky – a beautiful day for golf.

Our fourth was a few minutes late, and it was Steve who first noticed him as he walked up. "Oh great," he muttered to us. "Get a load of this."

We turned to see a tall, thin teenager approaching the tee box. He shouldered a worn-out golf bag and was sporting a prominent tattoo on his arm that complemented his four-inch, neon-yellow Mohawk. Sure enough, this character was our fourth.

He shouldered a worn-out golf bag and was sporting a prominent tattoo that complemented his four-inch, neon-yellow Mohawk.

"I do not need this today," moaned an exasperated Steve.

"Why do they even let kids like this on the course?" added Ed.

Still a few yards behind us, the kid yelled, "Y'all go ahead and hit. Let me swing for a couple of minutes to warm up."

"Like that's gonna help," Ed said under his breath. "This could be a very long round."

The three of us took turns teeing off and each of our drives on the first hole was respectable enough. All of our shots landed in the fairway, about 250 yards away. The compliments were flowing: "Good ball." "Nice shot." "That'll play."

Then we turned to let our fourth come up and drive and were shocked to see that he was still 30 yards behind us, teed up two boxes away, where the professionals play.

When his club hit the ball, it sounded like a cannon. We followed the flight of the small white sphere straight toward the trees, but rather than drop out of the sky like our shots, the ball continued to rise, cutting the corner and landing in the fairway at least 75 yards closer to the green than any of our shots.

While Ed and Steve pulled away in their cart, I waited to share my cart with our newest companion. He loped over, plopped his bag on the back of the cart, and sat down next to me.

"Great shot!" I said, truly meaning it.

"Hit it a little thin," he said. "But thanks."

In the fairway, the three of us hit approach shots on or near the green and then watched as this kid dropped a wedge to six feet from the hole. Then after about 20 minutes of watching us chip and putt, he stepped up and drained his birdie putt.

It was more of the same on Hole 2: a second birdie for the Mohawked kid, who clearly had a knack for golf despite a less-than-conservative look not often seen on the links. Needless to say, Ed and Steve started chatting it up with him, wanting to know what driver he was using, his thoughts on putters, what his best score was.

As he sat down next to me to ride over to the third tee, he grinned and said, "I hope I don't slow them down too much."

I laughed and said, "I don't think that will be a problem, son. Nice birdie. Mom would have loved watching that one! You'll have to tell her about it at lunch when we're done."

Yep, that tattooed, crazy-haired star golfer was Logan, my son, at the time a junior in high school and on a number of junior PGA tours. Beyond his stellar abilities on the green, he was also the co-founder of a nonprofit organization and had already literally traveled around the world to build deep-water wells in African villages. Oh, and he's just about the nicest kid you'll ever meet (and that's not just a proud papa speaking up. He *really is* just about the nicest kid you'll ever meet.).

Navigating The Generational Divide

On the golf course that day, Ed and Steve almost missed getting to know Logan and what he could do. Why? Because, thanks to their negative thinking, they assumed the worst about a teenager sporting a crazy hairstyle and a tattoo.

In previous generations, and in cultures all over the world outside of the United States, it's not uncommon for three generations or more to live under one roof. It was (and still is) the same way for Native Americans, who view their elderly as valuable, wise assets to their communities. But over the years, our modern-day, Western society's viewpoint has shifted. It's not nearly as common for aging family members to live in the same household with their children anymore; instead, an entire industry has grown up around facilities that house and care for them.

In further illustrating the disconnect between generations, I'm reminded of one commercial in particular – you may have seen it, too – where a teenage girl is sitting, solo, in front of her computer. She says after reading (the majority of) an online article about older people becoming more antisocial, she encouraged her parents to find more friends on Facebook, but they only have a mere 19. She, on the other hand, has 687 friends on Facebook – which, she says, constitutes "living," and proceeds to coo over an online post about a puppy that may or may not be real because it's "too small to be a real puppy."

Her parents, meanwhile, are carving up the trails on their mountain bikes with a few buddies. The commercial is advertising an SUV (the one the "friendless" parents drove, of course), but its humorous message also has a heavier undercurrent: a society that's becoming increasingly polarized on the age spectrum thanks, in large part, to technology.

Speaking in general terms of course *(this is not to say you feel exactly this way about your great Aunt Gertrude)*, younger generations tend to view older generations as outdated, slow, ignorant, and unworthy. The older generations, by the same token, often look down upon their younger counterparts as spoiled, lazy, too obsessed with technology, disrespectful, and – as I witnessed with Ed and Steve's first meeting of Logan – just plain crazy.

Leaders hold off on making snap judgments about others.

These are age-based stereotypes, and there are many more ways we prejudge people: based on their race, culture, social upbringing, or (something I see fairly often in the South) which college they went to. Obviously, buying into these types of stereotypes is dangerous, especially when it comes to developing your leadership and influence skills. Leaders hold off on making snap judgments about others based on preconceived notions. In today's society, which is becoming increasingly global, cross-cultural, and cross-generational, leaders let people prove themselves on the basis of merit, their contributions to the team or project, character, skills, experience, and abilities.

What?!? No Chocolate?!?

Have you ever known someone who, whenever they open their mouth, something negative comes out? I just want to smack people like this: the whiners, the complainers, the naysayers. It doesn't matter what the setting is, they will find something to complain about, grumble over, or belittle. These are the people who could have been given tickets to the Super Bowl on the 50-yard line and then complain that the sponsor logo in the center of the field is facing the other direction. They scratch off a lottery ticket that they bought on a whim to find they won $10,000 and then gripe about how much tax they'll have to pay. They get assigned a plum project at work and then wonder why it wasn't forthcoming a year ago.

I don't have many pet peeves, but these kinds of people top the list. And as I wrote the first draft of this very paragraph, one of them had been sitting a few tables away from me, in a nice little restaurant in Morgantown, West Virginia. This place's surf-and-turf buffet is a weekly hotspot and the night I was visiting, it was packed.

The griper in question was a real piece of work. This woman had been grumbling for 10 minutes that there was nothing chocolate on the dessert portion of the buffet. Her tirade went something like this: *"Can you BELIEVE there is nothing chocolate here! You pay this kind of money and you certainly expect to have at least ONE chocolate item! This buffet has certainly gone downhill since the last time I was here. Seriously, what a joke. NO CHOCOLATE!"*

Clearly, this woman's dinner companions got fed up with her and just wanted her to shut her (non-chocolate-eating) pie hole. I watched their evening slowly dissipate from a nice gathering with friends to frustration and embarrassment for the entire table.

Eventually they left, and I have to admit, hearing all that talk about chocolate put me in the mood for some, too. So I decided to ask my waiter (who was a different one than the poor fellow who had been serving the chocolate-deprived customer) about the possibility.

"Let me see what I can do for you," he said, and even asked whether I'd like chocolate cake or ice cream. I can't remember which one I chose, but a few minutes later he returned with them both anyway. I sat there eating my dessert, wondering what kind of rage that woman would have gone into had she seen me enjoying my chocolate mini-feast.

What I find so amazing is that many times the very things people are complaining about are things *they could actually do something to correct*. But, like the woman in the restaurant, instead of taking action to rectify the situation, they prefer to grumble and whine. And consider this: It takes the same amount of effort to whine and grumble to your dining companions about the lack of chocolate on the buffet as it does to ask your server if, perhaps, there is a way to snag a piece of chocolate cake or ice cream from the kitchen – as my little unscientific experiment illustrated.

Atmospheres Don't Just Happen

The first few days of school at the Ron Clark Academy in southeast Atlanta are unlike the first few days of school anywhere. A band plays as new students are welcomed into the building, along with high-fives and hugs from the entire staff. Teachers introduce themselves by whizzing down a twisting, two-story slide in the atrium. Students are assigned to one of four "houses" they'll call home for the following year, a tribute to the popular Harry Potter books and movies.

Then, for the next three days, students are not allowed to talk, except at lunch or when they are answering questions. Among the other requirements at RCA: Sunday best attire for staff and students, good manners and firm handshakes, and an unwavering philosophy of hard work and earned rewards.

Founder Ron Clark, who's considered one of the most successful educators of his time, describes his school as simultaneously the most magical and the strictest in the country. It's also one of the most successful, with more than 400 students applying for 30 spots every year, and thousands of hopeful teachers vying for training there. By just about any educator's account, RCA and its founder are superb models of how to inspire students to achieve levels of academic and personal success that they never thought possible.

Atmospheres don't just happen. Something causes an environment to be that way.

Of course, such an uplifting, motivational atmosphere didn't happen by accident. After turning around the performance of a seriously struggling class of students in East Harlem, Clark returned to his native South to build his dream school as a reflection of the principles he believes are essential to instill in today's students. RCA's unique environment didn't just happen by spontaneous combustion: It's the result of years of research, observation, input from experienced educators, and, of course, Clark's exemplary techniques.

It's the same in any other setting, whether it's within a school, office, restaurant, church, or even a family room: *Atmospheres don't just happen.* Whether they're good or bad, motivational or mellow, uplifting or one big downer, encouraging or stifling, something *causes* an environment to be that way.

Consider, for a moment, a place where you spend a lot of time. It could be your workplace, or church, or even your home. It can be a non-physical space, too: Perhaps involvement with a local running group or a knitting club. Now, think about the atmosphere in that environment and your mood when you're immersed in it. How would you describe it? Joyful? Content? Anxious? On edge? Satisified? Dissatisfied? Unhappy?

Even more importantly: Can you identify what role you play in creating or maintaining that environment? Even if you can't identify what it might be, I promise you have more influence than you think.

Emotional Contagion

We've all been there: Working or interacting on a regular basis with someone who always seems to suck everyone around them into a vortex of negativity. The tension, the underlying nasty currents, the whole vibe of the office, meeting, conference call, dinner table, wherever – just seems to shift the wrong way whenever they're around. It's like they bring a black cloud with them that darkens the atmosphere around them, too.

And over the past decade, scientific research has supported what everyone who's ever regularly been in the presence of such a person has known in their gut: That emotions and attitudes are contagious – especially bad ones.

Consider a 2005 study done by University of New Hampshire researcher Richard Saavedra, in which he and other researchers examined the effects of leaders' moods on groups. They selected 189 volunteer undergrads and divided them into 56 groups, telling them they were participating in an exercise to build team unity and cohesion.

Before the exercise, however, a "leader" chosen from each team was shown one of two video eight-minute clips: one of David Letterman, or a portion of a television documentary on social injustice and aggression. Each clip was designed to induce a positive or negative mood. All team members' moods were measured before and after the task, and the results showed that the leaders' moods permeated and influenced the mood of the group, with the negative moods (i.e., those that resulted from viewing of the torture clip) trumping the positive ones.[11]

Another researcher, Sigal Barsade of Yale's Wharton School of Business, has given a name to this phenomenon: emotional contagion. According to Barsade, when people are "infected" by the moods of others – especially their leaders – it impacts not just their own moods, but also their beliefs and even decisions they make.

And guess what inspired Barsade's pioneering research? A not-so-pleasant experience with a co-worker. Before attending graduate school, Barsade worked with a group that included a bad-tempered woman. But Barsade assumed that since she wasn't working closely with this woman, she had no real effect on her own life or outlook. However, once the crabby co-worker went on vacation, she noticed that the atmosphere of the group became much more pleasant, sociable, and enjoyable. When the grumpy gal returned from vacation, the atmosphere became tense and uptight once again.

Emotions and attitudes are contagious – especially bad ones.

As journalist Marina Krakovsky reported in a publication from the Wharton School of Business, Barsade said of that experience: "I remember how striking it was. It wasn't that she was telling us what to do, but just the way she was in the workplace that was influencing others."[12]

Let me repeat those words: *It wasn't that she was telling us what to do, but just the way she was in the workplace that was influencing others.*

Barsade's observations, and her breakthrough research, underscore the importance of leaders to understand how they can harness the inherent power of their own mood for greater good, whether it's in the office, at home, or interacting with a stranger in the coffee shop. When leaders learn to consciously take control of their own emotions – and the hard-wired influence those emotions have on others – they can serve as a powerful instigator for positive change in any environment.

You Get What You Tolerate

When we simply stand back and put up with negative environments or atmospheres and the behaviors that can cause them to flourish, whether that involves unprofessionalism or racism or rudeness, it's on us as leaders – *even if we don't have the formal title of one* – to take a stand. To react. To speak up. To do or say something to address and fix (or start addressing and fixing) the problem.

But I don't like to rock the boat!, you may be thinking. *I don't want to be a tattletale or part of office politics!*

Fine. But don't expect for things to change much, either. Why? Because *you get what you tolerate.*

By our definition of Leadership Redefined, if we do not try to influence a negative situation to make it better, we'll keep getting what we've been getting. This concept doesn't just apply to the workplace, either. You get what you tolerate in all aspects of life: marriages, relationships with children and other family members, friendships.

Leaders act as thermostats, not just thermometers.

Leaders have their ears finely tuned for that kind of call to action – even though it might sound more like a murmur because it's the status quo, the assumed path, the traditional "way we do things around here."

Leaders, however, understand that they have the power to be active, not just passive, in the face of an undesirable atmosphere. Put another way, they act as thermostats.

Consider how a thermometer works: by registering body temperature and then providing a reading. Now, think about a thermostat. This nifty little device (which, in my house, works overtime in the blazing Southern summer months) not only gauges the temperature of the surrounding air, it regulates it and cools or heats the room as necessary to maintain a comfortable environment.

It's a handy little analogy to how the best leaders operate: like thermostats. Not only do they register the temperature of their surrounding environment (by Examining Everything, remember) – they take the initiative to act, to influence the environment and move it where it needs to be.

Be A Balanced Optimist

When we're faced with a problem, challenge, or disappointment, it's natural to feel defeated, negative, or just plain ticked off. But, as you've no doubt heard before, a perpetually pessimistic attitude can wreck any hopes you have for happiness or success, regardless of which area of your life – work, family, friends, relationships – you're focusing on. Get stuck in a negative rut, and the negativity has the potential to sour everything you do.

This is another one of those times when I can almost hear what some of you are thinking: *But, Dave, I'm not gonna win any Pollyanna awards. I just don't think I can be happy and positive and optimistic all the time.*

That's ok.

I am a big fan of learning how to become a balanced optimist. A balanced optimist doesn't walk around with a perma-grin plastered on his face, giving the thumbs-up to everyone he sees in the hallway. A balanced optimist doesn't sugarcoat the challenges, problems, or pitfalls; he or she acknowledges them and finds a way to look at them as bumps in the road along the way to the final goal. Many leaders have learned how to become balanced optimists: realistic about the challenges, and determined to achieve success despite (or, perhaps because) of them.

Let's talk about a few simple strategies you can use to become a balanced optimist.

Use positive language. In terms of leadership, using positive language is critical, and to illustrate how powerful words can be, please follow the instruction below:

DO NOT THINK ABOUT
A PINK ELEPHANT.

What's the first image that popped into your mind? I'd wager that it's a pink elephant, despite the fact that I just instructed you *not* to think about a pink elephant.

Yes, my instructions were clear, but they actually prompted the opposite outcome. As leaders, we must learn to use words that do a better job of prompting our desired outcome by using positive language. Often, it's a simple reframing of direction. For example, picture yourself speaking to a six-year-old child and trying to convey a life-saving piece of information. If you tell that child:

DON'T RUN OUT INTO THE STREET!

... what is the image in his or her mind? Yes, it's *running out into the street*. Instead we should say:

WHEN YOU GET TO THE CORNER, STOP.

Now the image in the kid's mind is stopping before he reaches the street. Cool, huh? Understanding this concept and implementing this kind of communication could actually save kids' lives. (And, considering that studies show that 85 percent of messages from adults to children are negative – as in, "No, stop that!" or "Don't play with your food!" – using positive language could also help shape our kids into happier, more confident children.)

Simply reframing a desired outcome also can enhance office dynamics, family relationships, and virtually any interaction you have in your daily life. As parents, managers, teachers, and friends we must use words that create accurate pictures in the minds of others of what our desired outcome is. It sometimes helps to talk in pictures, as with the "don't run into the street" example above. To do that, try to frame the objective in terms of the goal with which it's aligned: making a great presentation, completing the project, reaching a sales goal.

Neutralize negativity. Everybody has had the (dis) pleasure of working with a chronic complainer at some point or another. You know the type: They always have to throw in their two cents on an issue, point out every little shortcoming, and nitpick ideas to death. Lots of fun to be around, right?

Well, over the years I've realized that, when confronted with these lovely individuals, one particular phrase seems to do a pretty decent job of shutting them up while freeing up critical brain space so you can direct your energy on making progress on whatever goal or project you're working toward.

Here it is (are you ready?): "Thanks for your input. I'll take it into consideration."

I like this one because it's simple, effective, polite, and true. If the commenting person (or people – sometimes they tend to travel in packs) does have a legitimate concern or complaint, now you know about it, and you will, as you say, take it into consideration. Either way, mission accomplished.

Eliminate negative self-talk. We all have that little voice in our heads. Ignore or stifle the nasty things it says and replace them with positive ones.

Recognize the difference between thinking *I want things to change* and *I want to change things*. The difference is *you* – playing an active, not a passive, role.

Celebrate the success and happiness of others. Negative energy is jealous, but positive people – leaders – are thrilled when others succeed. Use someone else's success as a motivator to make you a better person.

EXPLORE ON YOUR OWN

1. Think about the last time you let negative thinking affect a situation. What happened as a result? How could a different frame of mind have changed things?

2. Identify an upbeat, positive person in your life. How do they tend to make you feel when you hang out with them?

3. Identify someone with a negative outlook on life. How do you tend to feel after hanging out with them?

4. What is an area in your life in which you seem to have an overabundance of negative thinking? What are you focusing on? What should you be focusing on instead?

5. Have you ever had someone make a faulty snap judgment of you? How did that make you feel?

6. Think of a time when your own negative thinking may have caused you to completely misread someone before you even had a chance to get to know them. How can you try to prevent that from happening again?

7. Rather than complain about something (at home, at work, at church, at your health club, etc.), what are some other ways you could handle the situation?

8. Understanding that atmospheres don't just happen, that something causes them to be what they are, think about a situation in your life that you are not fond of. What are you doing to create or maintain that atmosphere? What could you do to improve it?

9. Realizing that you get what you tolerate, identify an aspect of your life in which you are tolerating something unpleasant. How would you like that situation to be? What do you need to do differently to make that happen?

10. Since everyone can operate as a thermometer and identify what is going on around them, how can you operate as a thermostat and change things?

11. Is there an area in your life in which you are focusing on the problems, challenges, and barriers instead of the cure, solution, or answer? Describe it.

12. Identify an example where you can genuinely celebrate the success and happiness of someone else. Now, go do it!

CHAPTER 7

EXPLORE ALL POSSIBLE AVENUES

Think left and think right and think low and think high.
Oh, the thinks you can think up if only you try!
~ Dr. Seuss

A widely used exercise to demonstrate the power of Exploring All Possible Avenues is the 9 Dot Challenge. You may have seen or tried it before. Here's how it works: In the image below, try to connect all nine dots using four straight continuous lines without lifting your pen off the page or tracing over a line you have already drawn. You can cross over a line but not retrace over it.

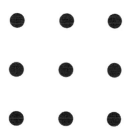

Did you solve the puzzle? Be honest – if you were able to complete the task, had you seen the answer before? Most people are unable to solve the 9 Dot Challenge. *(Heck, even folks who have seen the answer sometimes forget the solution!)* It's not obvious at first, but a look *beyond* the obvious often helps.

Let me give you a hint: If you're like the majority of people who attack this challenge, you probably tried to keep your lines within the boundaries of the nine dots. But the instructions do not mention anything about boundaries. So, try again, realizing that you can run your straight lines beyond the borders of the nine dots.

Did my hint help you? If so, way to go! If not, don't feel bad – I struggled with it, too. (Turn to page 144 to see the completed exercise.)

If you were unable to complete the challenge, consider this: Most people don't conquer it because they assumed that the nine dots formed a square or box with boundaries that could not be crossed. Therein lies the one of the great benefits of Exploring All Possible Avenues: It challenges people to open their minds, to look at things differently, to "think outside the box" (maybe this is where that phrase came from?).

Unconventional Answers

The following is an example of someone who has a knack for looking at things differently. Different versions of it have floated around the internet, and it appears to be pop quiz from a junior high school class, testing students on their general knowledge and critical thinking skills.

- **Q: In which battle did Napoleon die?**
  A: His last battle.

- **Q: Where was the Declaration of Independence signed?**
  A: At the bottom of the page.
- **Q: The Colorado River flows in which state(s)?**
  A: Liquid.
- **Q: If it took eight men 10 hours to build a wall, how long would it take four men to build it?**
  A: No time at all, because the wall is already built.
- **Q: If you had three apples and four oranges in one hand and four apples and three oranges in the other hand, what would you have?**
  A: Very large hands.

How different people view these answers can range all over the board. Teachers would probably see them as smart-alecky. Teenagers would probably see them as hilarious. But regardless how you view the answers, they're not wrong.

This is a critical skill for leaders: learning to Explore All Possible Avenues. Exploring All Possible Avenues is about opening your mind to options, solutions, or strategies that may not seem obvious at first. It's a close cousin to Examining Everything, but it's more action-oriented. When leaders Explore All Possible Avenues, they widen their perspective so they can take right, appropriate action, make the best decision, or affect the most positive outcome. They're considering a solution – or, an avenue – that may seem a little too far out there, just a tad off the wall or, believe it or not, far too simple.

Exploring All Possible Avenues is about not conforming. It's about challenging assumptions. It's about seeing things in a new way, which can help create positive outcomes, solve problems, and rise above challenges, no matter how insurmountable they may seem at first. It's about thinking differently, questioning traditional perspectives, and engaging in break-through solutions to problems or challenges you face. This kind of shift can lead to transformational change in your professional and personal lives, while greatly increasing your influence on those around you.

When Jim Lovell's voice crackled through to Mission Control just three days into the lunar mission *Apollo 13* saying, "Houston, we have a problem," it marked the beginning of one of the most remarkable lessons in leadership, conflict management, innovation, and unwavering determination that the world has ever seen. Today, Lovell's original warning, "Houston, we have a problem," has become a colloquialism for announcing that something isn't going according to plan.

But the real beauty of the *Apollo 13* story is the inspiration, creativity, and innovation that happened when the plan went agonizingly awry. Every single person involved in the endeavor, from the flight engineers at Mission Control to the astronauts orbiting the earth 200,000 miles away, committed to the mandate that "Failure is not an option," as demanded by mission control director of operations Gene Kranz.

And the entire team Explored All Possible Avenues to achieve that goal. To this day, *Apollo 13* is known as a "successful failure" for bringing all three astronauts safely back to earth, against nearly every conceivable obstacle – one of which was the problem of excess carbon dioxide in the module. In another feat of engineering genius, the team created a contraption to rid the module of carbon dioxide, using only the tools and equipment the crew had on board. As Jim Lovell wrote in his book *Lost Moon: The Perilous Voyage of Apollo 13:* "The contraption wasn't very handsome, but it worked."

Coconuts, Cacti, And A Corporate Slogan

People in sales must constantly Explore All Possible Avenues in hitting their numbers. In one of our Weber Associates sales schools, we teach sales reps this principle in a slightly different way. It goes like this: "Options unconsidered can never be exercised." It is the idea that many times we are the ones who limit our own problem-solving and, as we think in unconventional, different, and creative ways, new solutions can bubble to the surface.

Dan Seidman, the aforementioned author of *The Death of 20th Century Selling,* discusses how he used two items that are pretty uncommon in the workplace – a coconut and a cactus – in order to break through to two critical contacts within his sales accounts.[13]

With the coconut, Seidman was targeting a CFO he'd been trying to get an appointment with for two months. On the verge of giving up, he remembered a sort of tropical telegram: a Hawaiian company that would write a desired message on a coconut in black marker and then mail it to the desired recipient. He chose the words "You're a tough nut to crack," the coconut was sent, and Seidman hoped for the best.

Options unconsidered can never be exercised.

A week later, the CFO called, laughing over the coconut, and asked when he'd like to come in for a meeting. He used a similarly unique strategy with the cactus. He needed a government employee, who was known in her field as a prickly type, to help file some documents immediately.

Upon his initial request, she started shaking her head. But then he presented the potted succulent from behind his back

139

and said, with a smile, that he'd heard she was a hardworking type who most people didn't want to rub shoulders with, and that this was a little gift that reflected her personality.

That broke the ice of the worker's tough exterior, and she laughed and took care of the filing immediately.

One company, Taco Bell, has even riffed on the popularity of think outside the box as a corporate catchphrase. With its "Think Outside the Bun" slogan, the fast food giant encourages customers to remember that hamburgers aren't the only way to satisfy a fast-food craving.

Slam Dunks And Unconventional Successes

I am writing these words in March, and to the delight of basketball fans across the country and the world, March Madness is in full force. And just like every year as the season comes to a close, I'm reminded of the amazing feat accomplished by the UCLA Bruins during their unprecedented 10 NCAA Men's Basketball Championships, from 1963 to 1975.

During that amazing run, the University of California at Los Angeles had a number of truly talented players but arguably the best was Kareem Abdul-Jabbar. He was then known as Lew Alcindor, a shortened version of his given name, Ferdinand Lewis Alcindor. Alcindor's athleticism and ability to dunk made him almost untouchable on the court, and as of the publishing of this book, he still holds or shares a number of individual records at UCLA.

The NCAA Rules Committee made a rule change forbidding the dunk shot.

Those figures are even more impressive when you consider that between Alcindor's sophomore and junior years, the NCAA Rules Committee made a rule change forbidding the dunk shot.

It was widely believed that the committee had instituted this change to reduce Alcindor's dominance during games.

At first, Alcindor was devastated. He perceived the new rule as a huge barrier to his success, a giant obstacle thrown in his path. But his coach, the legendary John Wooden, challenged his perspective and told his star player to look at this barrier as a catalyst to Explore All Possible Avenues, and instead of seeing it as an obstacle, see it as a way to raise his game to a higher level.

As he later wrote in his autobiography, *Kareem:* "At the time, Coach Wooden told me it would only make me a better player, helping me develop a softer touch around the basket. This I could use to good advantage in the pros, where I could also, once again, use the dunk shot. He was right. It didn't hurt me. I worked twice as hard at banking my shots off the glass, on turn-around jump shots, and on my hook. [This barrier] made me a better all-around player."

Use obstacles and barriers as catalysts to help you Explore All Possible Avenues,

Just as the "no dunk" rule caused Alcindor to develop more of his potential by forcing him to Explore All Possible Avenues and focus on other skills and abilities, so too can challenges you face have the same positive impact on your life.[14]

Edison's Fire

The great American inventor Thomas Edison is widely known for his creative genius and innovative mind; in other words, for his Explore All Possible Avenues mentality. Edison was believed to have tried thousands of different ideas in his search for fila-ment in a light bulb, and his tireless exploring led to the birth of an invention that changed the world as we know it.

What you may not realize about Edison's story, though, is that his laboratory and plant were decimated by fire at one point. During the night of December 9, 1914, an inferno destroyed 10 separate buildings where Edison worked, causing damage estimated at $5 to $7 million – that's a lot of money today, let alone a century ago! But sadly, because the buildings were made of concrete and thought to be fireproof, they were only insured for $2 million.

As firemen battled the blaze that night, Edison's 24-year-old son Charles frantically searched for his father among the chaos. Finally, he found him calmly watching from a safe distance, his hair blowing in the wind and his face glowing in the reflection of the fire.

"My heart ached for him," Charles said. "He was 67 – no longer a young man – and everything was going up in flames."

Indeed, a majority of the great inventor's life's work was incinerated that December night. Can you imagine what must have been going through his mind?

Barriers can be the catalysts to achieving your true potential.

Sadness at his huge loss? Fear for what would happen to him? Anger at the insurance company for not properly assessing the buildings beforehand? Worry about the 7,000 employees whose jobs were now gone?

The following morning as the sun came up, Thomas Edison had indeed Explored All Possible Avenues as to how he would react, and while he could have chosen any number of options, he chose to respond by saying: "There is great value in disaster. All our mistakes are burned up. Thank God we can start anew."[15]

Edison's actions impart a powerful lesson: Whether the obstacle you face is new technology, a new competitor, a challenging student, or an economic downturn – or even a disaster like a fire – barriers can be the catalysts to achieving your true potential by pushing you to Explore All Possible Avenues.

Doing Things Differently

"We've always done it this way."
"This is how we handle things around here."
"That won't work."

Everybody has heard some version of this statement at some point in their lives. Such statements are the enemy of Exploring All Possible Avenues – and, unfortunately, what we sometimes perceive as reality.

Leaders tend to see things differently.

As human beings, it's impossible for us to view the world exactly as it is. How we see things around us stems from our ingrained beliefs, assumptions and perceptions that we don't examine (sound familiar?) or question. Those assumptions and beliefs may not match up with reality. Furthermore, such limitations tend to "box" us in and keep us closed off from different ways of processing information, solving problems, and associating with others. Such thinking resists change, desires conformity, stifles creativity, and dilutes the chances for success.

Leaders, however, tend to see things differently. They understand that their personal limitations and filters shape how they view the world – and that they need to get the whole picture. They understand that in order to think outside the box, they need to look beyond the obvious; in other words, that they need to Explore All Possible Avenues in order to achieve their goals and positively affect change.

(And speaking of thinking outside the box, here's the solution to the 9 Dot Challenge).

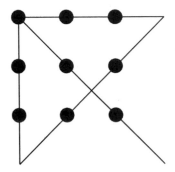

Blind Spots

While Exploring All Possible Avenues comes naturally to some people, it must be learned by others.

Fortunately, it can be.

Start with yourself, by taking a look into your blind spots.

We all have them. But I'm not talking about the areas on both sides of your car that you can't see into. I'm talking about the blind spots in our personalities, in our behaviors, in our character traits. The idea is the same, though: Just as there are areas on our vehicles that are obscured from our vision, that we can't see fully into, there are aspects of ourselves – the way we treat other people, how we relate and react to them, how we behave in certain situations and not in others – that we can't see into, either.

In fact, there's research to back this up. According to social psychologists, we humans are programmed to see others more clearly than we see ourselves. This phenomenon is called actor/observer differences.

Just like we have side mirrors that, if used properly, can help us see into the blind spots to better navigate our place on the road and enable us to get where we want to go, we have people around us who can help us see into our personal blind spots to better navigate our place in life and enable us to get where we want to go.

Who?, you might be thinking. *Which people in my life have the ability to reflect in such a way as to help me see into one of my blind spots?* Easy – it's the people who are around us and spend the most time with us: Our spouses and partners, friends, parents, colleagues, students, children. The keen observers, according to the aforementioned social psychologists, are those who are the closest to us. They have the ability to see better than we can into our own shortcomings and the areas and aspects of ourselves that we struggle with. They can use that third-person insight like a spotlight or microscope into our blind spot, illuminating and examining it.

We have people around us who can help us see into our personal blind spots.

The trouble is that it is not in our psychological makeup to solicit feedback from others on how we can become better. Sometimes, it's much easier not to see or examine what they see – especially when it's not pretty. So instead of gaining insight into some of our own shortcomings, we tend to focus on fixing other people's flaws.

For example, it is much easier to "help" my co-worker with her tendency to complain about the changes at work than it is to learn that I have a control issue and sometimes micromanage group projects. *Ouch! That kinda smarts, when I Explore All Possible Avenues and think of it that way!*

So, if it is not natural or easy for us to get help in dealing with our blind spots, how do we get started? How do we do it?

The Blind Spot Question

Let me share with you one of the most powerful questions possible to stimulate some honest communication in your life. I have seen this question, and the answers it triggers, transform marriages, offices, school departments, even parent/child relationships. And while the question seems simple (which it is), the power lies in the answer.

First off, a heads-up: This is a question to ask ONLY when the timing is right. Make sure you allow some time, at least half an hour, for some discussion. I don't recommend asking the question over the phone, or as you're about to board an airplane, or five minutes before you arrive at a dinner party with friends, or the annual sales meeting with your regional colleagues. Remember, the goal here is gaining some honest insight into yourself, of which you currently may be (and probably are) completely unaware.

So let's set the stage for asking the question with your significant other. You've gotten a sitter, a reservation, and a nice quiet table in your favorite restaurant. You sit down, grab your sweetie by the hand, and ask,

"What is the one thing you wish I would stop doing immediately?"

Take a deep breath and sit back a second as they digest what you've asked, which has opened yourself up to some potentially painful feedback. You see, whatever they answer at this point will be shedding light on something you are *currently* doing that they wish you were *not*.

No matter what the reaction – stunned silence, incredulousness, or even shedding a tear or two – that's the FIRST step, and it's the easy part. The next step is trickier: shutting your mouth and listening (which we discussed in Chapter 3). Remember, nothing new ever gets into your head through your open mouth. Don't argue. Don't disagree. Just listen.

The final step can be the most difficult of all: your response. You've asked the question and listened to the answer: Maybe it's that your life partner thinks you're not helping out enough around the house, or getting enough exercise, or spending enough quality time with your children. What *Nothing new ever gets into your head through your open mouth.* you choose to do in response will speak volumes as to the direction of that relationship and your willingness to change in order to improve it.

Or not.

If, over the next several days, weeks, or months, you and whomever you asked the question continue to discuss it (as well as what success looks like in this area) and you do, indeed, make changes, you are saying crystal clear, *I value you, and I want to be part of the solution and not part of the problem. Thank you for helping me be a better spouse/boss/friend. You are worth me making this change in our marriage/working relationship/friendship.*

If, however, you make no changes in this area and you disregard what was said, you are also sending a very clear message: *I may have taken the initiative to ask where I could*

147

improve on our relationship, but that's really about it. You're not worth the effort it would take for me to start making some changes. Get over it.

This question can be a catalyst to radically improve your relationships with others. Conversely, it can also send the relationship spiraling into friction, frustration, and even termination, based on your reaction to their answer. And it's not just a useful question for your relationship with your spouse, significant other, soul mate, or whatever you call your life partner, if you have one. This is a question that leaders learn to ask colleagues, coworkers, and kids too.

Many times it can be difficult for leaders to get honest feedback about their blind spots.

Through the insight I've learned from the Blind Spot Question, my kids have helped me become a much better parent. My employees have helped me to be a much better boss. But my improvements would have never come had I not asked the question in the first place. You see, many times it can be difficult for leaders to get honest feedback about their blind spots. After all, you're the leader – or, you're learning to become one! – and more often than not, people tend to say what they think you want to hear rather than shoot straight with you.

But by Exploring All Possible Avenues with the Blind Spot Question, you can start thinking and acting outside the box in a way that you never have before.

The Other Blind Spot Question

But what if you don't want to ask the question? What if you know what the answer would be and you're not quite ready to hear it verbalized? Well, that's ok...for now. You can start with another version of the Blind Spot Question I like to use:

What is the one thing you wish I would start doing immediately?

Rather than focus on your current negative behaviors, this question rephrases the issue in a softer way: what you are *not* doing that they wish you were.

People who are leaders Explore All Possible Avenues in order to improve themselves as human *beings* – not just human *doers*.

From Avenues To Action

So how can you intentionally move in the direction of Exploring All Possible Avenues? How can you influence breakthrough thinking from your colleagues, your team, your students, your kids?

First, have your group collectively identify and generate a list of all the assumptions behind the issue or problem at hand. Next, give everyone permission to challenge the assumptions in order to come up with different ideas. Third, have the group brainstorm and list as many ideas as they can come up with (with no judging or evaluating of the reality or feasibility of any of the ideas). Then, go through the process of evaluating the feasibility of the ideas. Lastly, prioritize the ideas and develop next steps. If the group feels confident to Explore All Possible Avenues and challenge the assumptions without fear of being punished in any way, you will find that – viola! – you have a list of potential new solutions.

Avenues For The Future

In closing, allow me to make something perfectly clear: Many times, it takes great courage to Explore All Possible Avenues, to think outside the box, to try things that have never been tried before. But just like we learned when discussing fear in Chapter 4, sometimes in order to get something you've never had, you must do something you've never done. And consider this: Do you know what the opposite of courage is? Not fear…that's what I used to think.

It's conformity.

The opposite of courage is conformity.

Continuing to do the same ordinary things will only lead to getting the same ordinary results. Be courageous, and Explore All Possible Avenues the next time you're faced with a challenge or bump in the road. And remember, it's easier to ask for forgiveness instead of permission.

That said, it's also important to remember parameters when you're Exploring All Possible Avenues. Josh Weston, chairman and CEO of Automated Data Processing Inc., puts it this way: "I've always tried to live with the following simple rule: Don't do what you wouldn't feel comfortable reading about in the newspapers the next day."

EXPLORE ON YOUR OWN

1. Were you able to complete the 9 Dot Challenge on you first attempt? If not, why? How do we do this with other challenges in our life?

2. Who, specifically, can you ask to help you see into the "blind spots" in your life at work? At home?

3. If you were to ask your [spouse/significant other/colleague/friend] the Blind Spot Question ("What is the one thing you wish I would stop doing immediately?"), how do you think they would answer? Consider both those people in your professional life as well as your personal life.

4. Do the same with the Other Blind Spot Question: "What is the one thing you wish I would start doing immediately?" How do you think they would answer?

5. Of the three steps identified in asking the above questions (asking the question, listening to the answer, and implementing the changes), which do you think will be the most difficult for you? Why?

6. In what setting or circumstance are you going to ask the question and to whom?

7. Identify a barrier, challenge, or obstacle in your life right now. Describe how you think about it. As you Explore All Possible Avenues, what might be some other ways to consider a solution to it?

CHAPTER 8

EXCEED NORMAL EXPECTATIONS & EXERCISE EFFORT

If you accept the expectations of others, especially
negative ones, then you never will change the outcome.
- Michael Jordan

About two years ago, I checked Churchill Downs off my bucket
list. My wife, Tina, daughter, Lindsey, and I went to Louisville, Kentucky, home of the celebrated "Run for the Roses,"
and we had a blast. The outrageous hats, the mint juleps, the
camaraderie, and, of course, the betting: It all made for an
unforgettable day.

Lindsey is a horse lover, and we were all mesmerized watching those beautiful creatures glide around the track. And
as exciting as they were, I couldn't help but looking at those
races and thinking that the winners, being determined "by
a nose," could be a metaphor for other things in life: specifically, how they represented a principle I like to call Exceed
Normal Expectations.

Consider the following:

- In order to get nearly twice the reward, did the first-
  place horse and jockey team have to run twice as fast as
  the other finishers?
- Did the horse have to run twice as far?

- Did the horse and jockey have to train twice as long?
- Did they even need to train twice as hard?

The answer to all four of those is no.

So, in order to reap the most glory (and money!) possible, how much better did the first-place horse have to be than the second-place horse?

Is there room in your life today to be just a nose better?

Just a nose.

Is there room in your life today to be just a nose better than the competition? Than you were yesterday? To move beyond the normal expectations that exist for you?

I would venture to say the answer to all of those questions is yes. So let's dig into how to Exceed Normal Expectations.

Exercise Effort (A Few Words On Hard Work)

Before we talk about what Exceeding Normal Expectations means, let me make note of the following: Making progress on purpose, which is an underlying philosophy of this book, requires hard work. Think about anyone who has achieved a certain level of success in some area of their life, whether it's the corporate world, education, sports, even raising their children. When asked how they got to that point in their lives, I'd say 99 percent of the time, they talk about all the hard work they put into it, all the blood, sweat, and tears.

What one can assume, then, is that those around them aren't doing as much.

And that's what Exceeding Normal Expectations is about. Although our notion of Leadership Redefined means that you're putting in a certain level of effort on your part, Exceeding Normal Expectations does not have to be a back-breaking, insurmountable challenge. It sometimes means doing *just a little bit better.*

Want more good news? There's no traffic jam on the extra mile. In other words, when you Exercise Effort in order to Exceed Normal Expectations, you'll find that not many others are traveling the road with you.

This principle is about taking those goals, dreams, and targets and putting action behind them. In other words, as an old Chinese proverb goes, "Great souls have wills. Feeble ones only have wishes."

A Salute To The Navy

I've given thousands of presentations during my 25-year career, but one that still stands out to this day happened in the summer of 2011. It was a presentation I made at the Naval Training Center in San Diego. It was my first opportunity to work with the fine service members of the United States military, and I was quite nervous. As I flew from Atlanta to southern California, I worried if the audience would enjoy my program and if my principles would apply to their world. I envisioned a room full of men and women in uniform, sitting at attention in perfect rows, staring back at me with hardcore expressions that conveyed, *"Hurry up, we've got a country to protect."* I mean, this was the home of the coveted Navy Seals training camp, where mere mortals are whipped into super-human levels of physical and mental toughness.

There's no traffic jam on the extra mile.

As always, I arrived early to make sure all the technology would cooperate. A little while later, the first sailors began to arrive, in uniform, sure enough – and I immediately felt out of place in my coat and tie. I'm not sure if they could "smell the fear" that I'm sure was radiating from me or not, but many of them came up and warmly introduced themselves. The first service members to arrive were actually part of the Navy Band that would play in front of the 200-strong crowd.

Incorporating this band was a first-class move that established a whole different atmosphere for a presentation. Countless times before, I've watched people trudge into a silent meeting or conference room like they were walking into a morgue. The dread in the room is almost tangible, and people often gravitate toward the back rows, already tuned out.

Everything is intentional.

But this day in San Diego was the opposite: With the lively tunes from the band filling the air, attendees cheerfully strode in, smiling at me. After an incredibly powerful performance of "The Star-Spangled Banner," I was introduced and took the stage in front of an eager, appreciative audience.

It was one of the best presentations I've given.

My contact told me later that the live band was just one of the logistical details in place to help make people feel instantly engaged; his exact words were, "Everything is intentional."

What a great lesson: the little, but intentional, things that can influence and make a big difference in our lives and our pursuits. What many people might have considered an afterthought – *"Hey, there was live music!"* – was actually an intentional step on the Navy's part in Exceeding Normal Expectations. It was all part of influencing and creating the best environment for learning to take place, one with positive energy that invited people to engage and get the most out of the experience.

Hats Off To Miss Hannah

But Exceeding Normal Expectations can exist on an individual level, too. Consider what happened to my daughter, Lindsey, on her very first day of school ever. My busiest time of year, as a professional speaker, is in August, which means I've had to miss many a first day of school while my children were young. But her first year, I was able to be a part of the experience with Lindsey by doing a "dry run" a few days beforehand.

I picked her up at the bus stop as the bus would, and we drove to school. Once we arrived, I parked where the bus would, and we walked into the school (and signed in, of course – don't even try to walk into a school these days without doing this!) and found Lindsey's classroom. We even made a trip to the cafeteria, where we simulated lunch, plastic trays and all. After our run-through, Lindsey was ready.

On the real first day of school, I was traveling, but I couldn't wait to talk to Lindsey and see how things went. I can't remember which city I was in, but I sure remember her excitement over the phone, especially when she started talking about Miss Hannah and how nice she was. *How grateful I am that my daughter has a teacher she loves so much,* I thought.

Not long after that, I had my first chance to go to Lindsey's school and check things out for myself. Lindsey was about to jump out of her skin to have me meet Miss Hannah. So I was a bit surprised when the teacher introduced herself by a name that was *not* Miss Hannah. *Hmm,* I thought, *maybe it's the assistant,* but nope, that wasn't her name, either. I was starting to get really curious about who Miss Hannah was, but I didn't say anything.

A little while later, I got my answer. Lindsey and I headed to the cafeteria and moved through the line. "Well, hello, Sunshine!" a bright voice boomed at my daughter.

"HI, MISS HANNAH!!" Lindsey beamed back at the lovely woman behind the counter. Mystery solved: Miss Hannah was the lady who served my daughter and all the other children lunch every day. In the grand scheme of the education system, her role may seem minimal, but I promise you the optimism and joy Miss Hannah brought to my daughter's education – and that of hundreds of other students, I'm sure – was immeasurable.

And Miss Hannah taught me a lesson that's brought profound insight to my life: People may not always remember what you did or what you said, but they'll always remember how you made them feel. Remember when you were a kid and, as you were under the weather, Mom's hand on your forehead would somehow offer comfort? It wasn't that she had magical healing powers of touch, but the simple act would convey such caring and compassion that it would perk your spirit.

> *People may not always remember what you did or what you said, but they'll always remember how you made them feel.*

It's the same idea with this new definition of what leadership means. Miss Hannah, for example, was a leader every day, simply by her smile and cheerful demeanor. For my daughter, and probably for dozens of other kids, she transformed an ordinary meal into a highlight of the day. By virtue of her positive attitude every day, she transformed an unlikely job position into a leadership role for education as a whole.

Practice Does Not Make Perfect

Think for a second what it would be like if every organization and individual Exceeded Normal Expectations like the Navy did that day of my presentation and Miss Hannah did with the students in her line at lunch. Indeed, when you come across people and groups who Exceed Normal Expectations, they stand out like a bubbling spring in a barren desert.

Consider, for example, an industry whose image these days is marred by flight delays, surly customer service staff, and ever-broadening fees: the airline industry. But at least one company, Southwest, has carved out a niche of thousands of dedicated customers because, unlike almost every other airline out there, it doesn't charge already-frazzled customers for their baggage. It also places an emphasis on its employees having fun, which is certainly evident in their attitudes. Once, I even found myself doubled over in laughter *(well, as doubled over as you can get in an airline seat)* as a Southwest lead flight attendant gave the safety talk as a stand-up comedy routine. Trust me, everyone was listening to every word he said, as opposed to texting, reading the paper, or even sleeping, which is more often than not the rule rather than the exception in those pre-flight announcements.

On an individual level, Exceeding Normal Expectations can be equally powerful. Think back a second to the bus driver and the administrative assistant from the beginning of this book. If they'd taken a minute to Exceed Normal Expectations, by making sure the sick boy was taken care of or directing his mother to the appropriate department, do you think they would have been looking for a new job the next day? I highly doubt it.

So how do you learn how to Exceed Normal Expectations? The key word is "habit." In order to consistently Exceed Normal Expectations, you have to make doing so a habit.

But most people have habits all wrong. As I mentioned earlier in this chapter, if you've ever heard anyone talk about excellence or greatness or being the best, they've probably mentioned all the long hours, the sacrifices, and the focus. While all those are true, there is usually one other factor that gets some airtime: practice, practice, practice. It is one of the most overused phrases of our time: "Practice makes perfect."

The phrase is most often heard in the sports arena, as coaches have hammered it into their athletes' heads for decades. Sales managers ingrain it into their sales reps. Math teachers have shared it with students. However, it's not exactly true. Practice does not make perfect – practice makes permanent!

I don't think I truly began to understand this principle until I had an in-person encounter with one of golf's great champions, Larry Nelson. Although Nelson didn't pick up a club until age 21, after serving in the Vietnam War, he won 40 professional golf tournaments, including two PGA Championships and a U.S. Open, throughout his incredible career.

One day, my son, Logan, heard that Nelson would be giving a free golf clinic prior to a charity golf tournament nearby. Logan, a very good junior golfer, burst into the house looking like he'd just downed a gallon of 5-Hour Energy, begging me to take him.

However, it wasn't a regular PGA event – it was a private fundraiser wherein a bunch of people sign up, pay a bunch of money, and play hooky from work to enjoy themselves on a golf course. I initially told Logan no, but as kids are wont to do, he wore me down. But I told him the only way we could see Nelson in action would be if we could find a way to sneak in and watch the clinic, because I had no intention of paying that kind of dough to get in.

So, very early the next morning, jumpy with nerves, we parked in the empty parking lot at the country club. We shouldered our clubs and walked toward the clubhouse, right past all the officials setting up registration, and out the back onto the driving range like we owned the place. We were in, and honestly, in that moment, whether we got to actually see Larry Nelson at the clinic was secondary to the glorious sense of Superdad pride I felt for getting us just to this point.

At the far end of the range, Nelson was crushing balls as he was warming up to teach the clinic. We walked closer, watching him work through all the clubs in his bag, hitting each several times and working the ball high, low, left to right, right to left. It was an amazing display of athleticism. After about 20 minutes, a crowd of about 40 people had gathered.

Practice does not make perfect - practice makes permanent!

At one point, I believe Nelson had a 9-iron in his hand, and we had all just witnessed him hit several shots into the exact same place: a sign with a giant 150 painted on, it indicating that it was 150 yards away. The shots kept coming – BANG! BANG! BANG! – and finding their mark, each time, every time. We spectators were shaking our heads in disbelief.

Well, as a professional speaker, I had been quiet for far too long. So I put on my best redneck voice and I asked out loud, "Hey Larry, whatcha aimin' at?"

Laughter broke the awed silence. It was such a silly question – obviously, everybody knew he was aiming at the 150-yard marker, right?

I almost fell over when Nelson stepped back, turned to me, and said, "The 5."

And in that moment everything changed. You see, I just thought he was warming up – you know, practicing. But he wasn't *just* practicing. He was practicing perfectly, by naming a very specific target and aiming for excellence every time he hit the ball.

Honing Good Habits

One of the most famous quotes from Aristotle is this: "We are what we repeatedly do. Excellence, then, is not an act but a habit."

Consider, then, the following:

- Did you teach 2nd period differently than 3rd period, when an evaluator was in your room?
- Do you talk on the phone to one customer differently than you do to another when your boss is standing over you?
- Do you use certain words when speaking to your children in the car on the way to church than you do inside the building 15 minutes later?

Good leaders don't have just the desire to be better; they have the discipline to push themselves toward excellence, whether someone is watching or not. If you have this book in your hands, it's a safe bet that you want to improve in one or more aspects of your life. The trick is making that effort the baseline – making the effort to Exceed Normal Expectations as often and as consistently as possible. It's about focusing on little improvements all along the way, small

Good leaders have the discipline to push themselves toward excellence, whether someone is watching or not.

corrections, tweaks, and adjustments that, over time, equate to significant improvement.

Ask yourself, as often as you can, questions like this:

- How can I interact with that person so they have the most positive feeling possible about my company?
- What can I do to make the other person's day better?
- What can I do to make the other person's day easier?
- How can I be a better team player?
- How would I rate my performance today as a parent, employee, friend, or spouse?
- Is it time to ask someone around me the Blind Spot Question?

The Smooth Sounds Of Marvin

Every time I travel and rent a car, I think about a very memorable man who Exceeded Normal Expectations in his job as a shuttle bus driver for a rental car company, an industry where I have limited interactions with humans these days. It happened a few years back, in Memphis, and I'd given three different presentations to three different clients in the same day. I was exhausted and happily headed home.

At the airport, I dropped off my rental car and boarded the shuttle to the terminal. As I climbed aboard, a deep, baritone voice greeted me. "Welcome to your escape from everything," it said. "Sit back, relax, and enjoy the sounds of some of the best jazz you have ever heard."

I looked at the bus driver, who was smiling and speaking into the microphone. "Let these notes carry you away to a peaceful place, an idyllic getaway. My name is Marvin, but you can call me Velvet because my voice and my ride are *smooooooth.*"

Needless to say, all the other bleary-eyed road warriors and I looked at each other with a shared *"Is he for real?"* expression. Oh, but Marvin was just getting started. He introduced each song on his CD. He gave interesting background information about the artists. He asked if we had any requests. He played mini-trivia games with us. He got us all interacting with him and each other.

It was amazing to watch. In less than 10 minutes, Marvin had transformed the same old boring shuttle ride with a bunch of tired strangers into a positive, upbeat, fun experience. As we exited, every single passenger thanked Marvin, who was already up on his feet to high-five us. He, in turn, thanked us all for choosing his company, wished us well, and asked that, when we returned, would we please allow him to serve us.

Thanks to Marvin, that was the single best rental car company experience of my life (and trust me, I rent a lot of cars). And the reason for my positive customer experience? Not the reservation specialist, not the counter agent who got me a map of the area, not the security guard who made sure I had the right vehicle and a full tank of gas as I pulled out of the lot. Nope. It was all about Marvin, the shuttle bus driver.

There is no such thing as an unimportant job.

Did I do business with that car rental agency after that? You bet. The next time I'm in Memphis, I'll probably even wait an extra few minutes if I can ride on Marvin's bus.

There is no such thing as an unimportant job. You have the ability, with whatever you do, to make it extraordinary, like Marvin did, by Exceeding Normal Expectations in every interaction, every day. With his smooth sounds, Marvin was – and probably still is – acting as a leader with every customer who stepped onto his shuttle bus.

Just Another Fare?

I'd like to leave you with the story of a taxi driver in a big city, which has floated around the internet for a while. By all accounts, this taxi driver Exceeded Normal Expectations in what he called the most important fare of his life.

I arrived at the address before dawn and honked the horn. After waiting a few minutes, I walked to the door and knocked. "Just a minute," a frail, elderly voice answered.

I could hear something being dragged across the floor. After a long pause, the door opened. A small woman who appeared to be in her nineties stood before me. She was wearing a print dress and a pillbox hat with a veil pinned on it, like someone out of a 1940s movie. By her side was a small nylon suitcase.

The apartment looked as if no one had lived in it for years. The furniture was covered with sheets. There were no clocks on the walls, no knickknacks or utensils on the counters. In the corner was a cardboard box filled with photos and glassware.

"Would you carry my bag out to the car?" the woman asked.

I took the suitcase to the cab and returned to assist her. She took my arm and we walked slowly toward the curb. She kept thanking me for my kindness.

"It's nothing," I told her. "I just try to treat my passengers the way I would want my mother treated."

"Oh, you're such a good boy," she said.

When we got in the cab, she gave me an address and then asked me to drive through downtown.

"It's not the shortest way," I answered quickly.

"Oh, I don't mind," she said. "I'm in no hurry. I'm on my way to a hospice."

I looked in the rear-view mirror. Her eyes were glistening. "I don't have any family left," she continued in a soft voice. "The doctor says I don't have very long."

I quietly reached over and shut off the meter. "What route would you like me to take?" I asked.

For the next two hours, we drove through the city. She showed me the building where she had once worked as an elevator operator. We drove through the neighborhood where she and her husband had lived as newlyweds. She had me pull up to a furniture warehouse that had once been a ballroom where she had gone dancing as a girl.

Sometimes she'd ask me to slow in front of a particular building or corner and would sit staring into the darkness, saying nothing.

As the first hint of sun was creasing the horizon, she suddenly said, "I'm tired. Let's go now."

We drove in silence to the address she had given me. It was a low building, with a driveway that passed under a portico. Two orderlies came out to the cab as soon as we pulled up. They watched her every move. They must have been expecting her.

I opened the trunk and took the small suitcase to the door. The woman was already seated in a wheelchair. "How much do I owe you?" she asked, reaching into her purse.

"Nothing," I responded.

"You have to make a living," she answered.

"There are other passengers," I said. Almost without thinking, I bent and gave her a hug. She held onto me tightly.

"You gave an old woman a little moment of joy," she said. "Thank you."

I squeezed her hand and walked into the dim morning light. Behind me, a door shut. It was the sound of the closing of a life.

I didn't pick up any more passengers that shift. I drove aimlessly, lost in thought. For the rest of that day, I could hardly talk. What if that woman had gotten an angry driver, or one who was impatient to end his shift? What if I had refused to take the run, or had honked once, then driven away?

On a quick review, I don't think that I have done anything more important in my life.

Every job, every interaction with another person, is a self-portrait of the person behind it. What do your interactions say about you – that you travel the same tired road as everybody else? No more! Intentionally Exceed Normal Expectations and choose to increase your positive influence on the much-less-traveled road to success.

Every job is a self-portrait of the person behind it.

EXPLORE ON YOUR OWN

1. Is there room in your life today to be a nose better than you were yesterday? How?

2. Name some ways that you could intentionally create a better environment to impact your work life.

3. Name some ways that you could intentionally create a better environment to impact your home life.

4. It is easy to sometimes think our role is not that important in the big scheme of things. How can you change the image you have of your job? What do you do to positively impact the lives of others?

5. How do you want people to feel as a result of interacting with you?

6. Do you perform certain roles differently based on who may or may not be watching? (Hint: Most of us do!) How can you develop the habit of always performing to the highest standards, no matter who (if anyone) is watching?

7. Identify an important area of your life where you sometimes just "go through the motions." How can you change your actions to improve that role?

CHAPTER 9

EXHIBIT AN ATTITUDE OF OPTIMISTIC CONFIDENCE

Leadership is a matter of having people look at you
and gain confidence, seeing how you react. If
you're in control, they're in control.

- Tom Landry

An exhausted and jet-lagged dad had just walked in from a brutal week of working and traveling across the country. As he was unpacking, his son burst into his bedroom carrying a baseball bat and ball and excitedly announced, "Dad, you have to see what a great baseball player I am now!"

"All right, son," the dad replied. "Just let me change my clothes first."

"Ok, but hurry! You are not going to believe your eyes! I am the greatest baseball player in the world!"

A few minutes later, the father followed his son into the backyard, where the little boy proceeded to rest the bat on his shoulder, throw the ball up in the air with his left hand, and then quickly grab the bat with both hands and swing as the ball came back down.

On his first attempt, the little boy completely missed the ball. Undaunted, he retrieved the ball, tossed it back up in the air, and swung again, missing. His dad was starting to get a little embarrassed for him and moved in to help.

"No, Dad!" his son said with a huge grin spread across his face. "One more time."

With a firm resolution he gripped the bat harder, tossed the ball up, and for the third time, swung the bat – and completely missed the ball.

His father's heart was breaking for his son when the little boy turned and excitedly pronounced, "Do you see what I mean?! I am a *great* pitcher! Unhittable!"

Optimistic Confidence Inspires

Like that little boy envisioned himself as an unhittable pitcher, leaders see themselves succeeding. They have the ability to look into the future and envision themselves obtaining their goal. Hitting their target. Achieving their dreams. And they can inspire others along the way. But this confidence is not just directed inward in the form of self-confidence. It must also be directed outward, to others. Leaders exhibit confidence in themselves – *and* in those around them. They have the ability to believe in others sometimes before others can believe in themselves.

After all, what good would it be if a sales manager had confidence in himself as a manager but none in his sales team to actually make the sale? What kind of an impact would a teacher have if she had confidence in her own ability to teach but none in her students' ability to learn? To exhibit an Attitude of Optimistic Confidence is to believe in the greatness that exists in everyone and to intentionally work to release that greatness toward a positive outcome.

But how do I do that?

Good question. Optimistic Confidence is primarily conveyed through three areas:

Leaders exhibit confidence in themselves - and in those around them.

- your body language (what you do and how you do it),
- your words (what you say), and
- your tone, pitch, vocal quality, and volume (how you say it).

From the bounce in your step, to the sparkle in your eye, to the words you choose, to the tone and pace with which you say them, to your gestures, taking a closer look at these elements can help you really improve your communication skills – and your positive influence on others in the process.

People who align all three of the above in a positive way can become incredibly contagious. Their positive demeanor and outlook begins to rub off on everyone they come into contact with. In fact, people who Exhibit an Attitude of Optimistic Confidence can have both a unifying and a galvanizing effect on those around them, putting them on the path to becoming leaders.

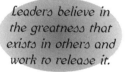

Leaders believe in the greatness that exists in others and work to release it.

To see this concept in action, simply consider some of the most popular films in Hollywood history. They're full of examples of leaders Exhibiting an Attitude of Optimistic Confidence, and the impact they have on others and the situations they find themselves in. From Mel Gibson inspiring his Scottish countrymen in *Braveheart* to Russell Crowe rallying a group of slaves fighting for their lives in the coliseum in *Gladiator* to Elliot and his bike-riding buddies getting E.T. to his spaceship as government scientists close in, Exhibiting an Attitude of Optimistic Confidence moves people to believe in a better outcome and take action toward it.

Off the big screen, I can think of no better example of someone who demonstrated optimistic confidence, even in the face of death, than the late Randy Pausch. A computer sciences professor at Carnegie Mellon University and a married father of three, Pausch was diagnosed in 2006 with terminal pancreatic cancer. He was given about six months to live.

Pausch's "Last Lecture" answered the question that had been posed to the annual speaker of a lecture series at Carnegie Mellon: What would you say if you knew you were going to die and had a chance to sum up everything that was most important to you?

Pausch's topic, "Really Achieving Your Childhood Dreams," an hour-plus-long lecture full of wisdom, humor, and heart-wrenching inspiration, was videotaped and put on the internet for the few friends, family members and colleagues who weren't able to personally attend his lecture in person. And, even among the constant online chatter, his powerful messages took hold. When this book went to press, Pausch's lecture had been viewed more than 14 million times on YouTube, and his lecture has become a runaway best-selling book as well.

As you Exhibit an Attitude of Optimistic Confidence, you inspire others to be better and do better.

Pausch died on July 25, 2008, having impacted millions of people with his inspirational message and attitude. Talk about looking at his situation as a glass half full: Pausch may have been more realistic than confident about his chances of survival – which were next to none – but his outlook was supremely positive, even as he was living the last few months of his life. It's been said on advertisements across the country (I've seen plenty in airports) that Pausch "wrote the book on living while dying," with a photo of him giving his last lecture.

Through his Attitude of Optimistic Confidence during not only his last lecture, but also his final months, Pausch became the catalyst that moved many others to finally take control of their lives and inspired them to really achieve their childhood dreams.

You see, that's the power behind this strategy. As you Exhibit an Attitude of Optimistic Confidence, you inspire others to be better and do better. Confidence can be contagious. Recognize that as a leader – someone who has influence – you can learn to intentionally and positively impact the lives of those around you regardless of your position. Randy Pausch was completely unknown to 99 percent of the people who have watched or read his "Last Lecture," but he influenced millions because of his optimistic confident outlook that his words were truth and worthy of being applied, *and* that his listeners had the ability within them to make the changes they needed to make.

Perhaps you're thinking, *Dave, I'm not a college professor with a few months to live, and I'm not leading people into battle or hangin' with aliens. I will not be giving a "Last Lecture" on YouTube. I really don't have a platform to try to positively influence the situation.* That's what is so great about this strategy – you don't have to be or have any of those!

Challenger Baseball

In *Chicken Soup for the Unsinkable Soul,* an essay by Darrell J. Burnett[16] describes a heartwarming story about an experience he had coaching developmentally disabled children in the Challenger Division, which was part of the Little League in Los Angeles.

Burnett calls his first game "an eye-opener" as he saw children in a range of ages with cerebral palsy, spina bifida, autism, and a variety of other developmental disabilities. However, Burnett notes, they had at least one thing in common: "they were having fun!" Every participant in a Challenger game

Exhibited an Attitude of Optimistic Confidence. They wanted to play ball and have fun, regardless of their ability or skill level.

You see, each Challenger player had a buddy to help them during the game, almost always a parent or sibling, who pushed a wheelchair or pointed which base to run to. But the stands, Burnett noticed, were almost empty.

It was a very different experience than what he'd seen during Saturday games, when the other kids played: parents screaming at the umpires, coaches yelling at the players, players crying from all the pressure on what was supposed to be a fun game.

Burnett writes that suddenly "it became clear to me how important it was to get Challenger games scheduled among the other Little League games – both for the exposure of the Challenger kids to the other kids, and for the lessons in sportsmanship and fun they could give the other kids and parents." And that's what he did, as manager of the Challenger Division the following season.

The results were phenomenal. Challenger games were integrated with the other ones, and able-bodied players on the 11- and 12-year-old division began to serve as buddies to the Challenger players. It was the first exposure some of them had with children with developmental disabilities, and they were a little hesitant at first, Burnett wrote. But after a while, the Challenger players' determination, hard work and optimistic "can do" confidence won them over. Plus, since the games were scheduled on the same day, the stands were full with parents of the able-bodied buddies, and the feelings of goodwill and inspiration from the Challenger game helped tame some of the nastiness that had been so rampant in the other games.

When the other kids played, parents screamed, coaches yelled, and players cried.

Burnett summed it up like this: "To see and feel the warmth of camaraderie and compassion on the baseball diamonds that day renewed everyone's faith in the goodness of the human spirit," he wrote. "Challenger sports created memories that whole season which will last a lifetime for those Challenger kids, those buddies, those parents, coaches, and spectators."

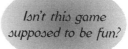
Isn't this game supposed to be fun?

But what if I'm not in a baseball league like that?, you may be wondering. *What if I can't even communicate very well?* Sorry, that still does not disqualify you from Exhibiting an Attitude of Optimistic Confidence and positively impacting the world around you. Anyone can do this, in any setting, at any time.

Read on for an example of someone who did just that when I met him years ago, and I'm sure is still doing so this very day.

Ben The Stutterer

It was a busy Monday morning as we welcomed two dozen managers to participate in one of our open-to-the-public Leadership Skills Workshops. Some of the most well-respected companies in America had sent their managers to Atlanta to get "Weberized." Typical for first day interactions at a program of this nature, the extroverts in the room were meeting everyone and conversations between participants centered mostly on their arrival into Atlanta.

At 8 a.m. we had participants take their assigned seats at the big "U" table configuration. While there are many different ways to begin a multi-day seminar like this, we decided to simply go around the room and have each of these leaders introduce themselves and give their company name and role in it.

Things were running smoothly until about halfway through, when it came time for Ben to introduce himself. As the others had done, he stood to his feet and began, "M-M-M-M-M-M-My name is B-B-B-B-Ben T-T-T-T-T-Thompson. I w-w-w-w-work at C-C-C-C-Caterpillar and I am in p-p-p-parts."

Ben, obviously, was a stutterer. And if I – as the workshop organizer – had known this ahead of time, I could have used so many other ways to have these folks introduce themselves to each other: activities, games, ice breakers. But no. I hadn't Explored All Possible Avenues in my preparation for the workshop, and so I'd put Ben on the spot by asking him to stand up in front of a roomful of folks he didn't know and speak with everyone staring at him.

David, you idiot, I thought to myself.

You can imagine the awkward tension that filled the room as everyone's heart went out to that poor guy. I honestly had no idea what to do.

But Ben did.

You see, he wasn't through with his introduction yet. He continued, "I w-w-w-w-would have said l-l-l-l-l-l-logistics, b-b-b-b-but I was afraid I would h-h-h-h-h-h-hurt myself."

You can imagine the awkward tension that filled the room. I honestly had no idea what to do.

Laughter exploded around the room, immediately diffusing the awkwardness. Ben began to bow to the crowd as if he had just completed an aria. As the laughter died down, he added, "B-B-B-B-But you should see me t-t-t-t-t-type!"

What a great example of Exhibiting an Attitude of Optimistic Confidence! In just a few moments Ben had completely transformed the situation from an embarrassed, awkward, "I just want to hide" moment into a positive, relaxed environment.

And in the process he even drew everyone in the room closer together. His actions created an atmosphere that permeated our entire week of learning, laughing, and transparency with those managers.

Consider The Alternatives

To understand the importance of Exhibiting an Attitude of Optimistic Confidence, contrast it with the alternatives: an attitude of lukewarm neutrality or, worse, pessimistic doubt. At their very best, these attitudes do not usually go hand-in-hand with success or achievement, and at their worst, they can actually derail, deflate, or even sabotage your own efforts and the efforts of those around you.

One of the most amazing studies I have ever seen with respect to the enormous potential impact of Exhibiting an Attitude of Optimistic Confidence was conducted by Dr. Elizabeth Hurlock and reported in the *Journal of Educational Psychology*.[17] Hurlock set out to see what impact, if any, could be traced back to the kind of feedback students received on their work.

She divided fourth- and sixth-grade students with the same math proficiencies as their peers into three groups. With the first group, she decided to Exhibit an Attitude of Optimistic Confidence. The second group would be comprised of students to which she would exhibit an attitude of pessimistic doubt. Finally, the third group would be confronted with an attitude of lukewarm neutrality (basically ignored). She wanted to see how, if at all, the students' performance in math would be impacted by her behavior toward them and their abilities.

On the first day, all the students were given a math assignment. Since they shared similar math proficiency, they all performed about the same. Keep in mind, however, that the students did not know they were at the same math proficiency as the other students, and their individual scores were not revealed to everyone. Additionally, the students did not realize that they had been secretly divided into three groups.

Upon grading the students' work, Hurlock Exhibited an Attitude of Positive Confidence as she showered the students in Group 1 with praise and affirmation. In front of the other two groups, she told this group how well they had done. She focused on all the correct answers they got, how many problems they had solved, basically communicating that they were superior to the other students. Her body language, her words, and her tone were in complete alignment. She communicated that she believed in these students and their abilities and, even though they had performed beautifully so far, that she was sure they could do even better! She helped to create an environment where their potential could be achieved.

How do you think those Group 1 students felt about themselves?

How do you think they felt about Dr. Hurlock?

How do you think they felt about math?

Now, the students in Group 2 had performed *exactly the same* as the students in Group 1 – but they didn't know it (remember, the grades were not revealed). With Group 2, though, she exhibited an attitude of pessimistic doubt. Again, in front of the other students, Hurlock publicly expressed her disappointment at their work and told them it was filled with careless errors. She focused on the problems they answered incorrectly and told this group they were inferior to the other students. She also said she didn't really feel confident that they could do math well.

How do think these Group 2 students felt about themselves?

How do you think they felt about Dr. Hurlock?

How do you think they felt about math?

Finally, with Group 3, even though these students had performed the same as all the other students, Hurlock completely ignored them. These students had heard her interactions with the other two groups, but she did not directly engage them at all.

Day after day this went on, and the results were startling. Even though the students had all started with the exact same math grades and proficiency, the students with whom Hurlock Exhibited an Attitude of Optimistic Confidence began to produce significantly better and better results than the students in the other two groups.

In other words, Hurlock's positive words and Optimistic Confidence created positive relationships, and her negative, pessimistic doubt bred negative relationships. Those relationships, in turn, began to impact the culture and attitudes among the students. As a result, some students were willing to work harder, while others began to perform more and more poorly. The correlation between words and results was astounding. Leaders understand the following progression:

Words impact relationships.

Relationships impact culture.

Culture impacts results.

Whether the setting is students in a classroom, colleagues tackling a major project at work, or overcoming some adversity in one's personal life, leaders understand that Exhibiting an Attitude of Optimistic Confidence is the ticket to success and happiness, both for themselves and those around them.

EXPLORE ON YOUR OWN

1. How can you Exhibit Optimistic Confidence in others with whom you interact on a regular basis?

2. Describe how misunderstanding or misperception can occur if you focus on *what* is said versus *how* it's said.

3. When you interact with someone who Exhibits an Attitude of Optimistic Confidence, how do you feel?

4. Name someone you know who displays Optimistic Confidence. Describe what they do that makes them that way.

5. Three movie examples were given in this chapter of individuals Exhibiting an Attitude of Optimistic Confidence: *Braveheart, Gladiator,* and *E.T.: The Extra Terrestrial.* Name another movie and describe a scene in which a character's Optimistic Confidence moved you.

6. Why do you think people are inspired to be and do their best when coming face to face with an Attitude of Optimistic Confidence?

7. The alternatives to Optimistic Confidence are lukewarm neutrality and pessimistic doubt. Have you ever encountered these in someone? How did it make you feel? Could you be the source of these attitudes and behaviors for another person? How could that impact them?

8. Who can you intentionally build up and affirm this week? How will you do it? Will this be difficult for you? Why or why not?

CHAPTER 10
EXTEND A HELPING HAND

We can't help everyone, but
everyone can help someone.

− Ronald Reagan

The Golden Gate Bridge in San Francisco is one of the world's great icons. Initially described as "the bridge that could never be built," this 1.7-mile span across the Golden Gate, as the geographical region in northern California is often called, is a testament to innovation, invention, and the power of the human spirit. It's one of the most popular tourist attractions in the world.

But many people don't know that this magnificent bridge, which celebrated its 75th anniversary in May 2012, also is one of the world's deadliest places. About 30 people commit suicide by jumping off it every year. That breaks down to about one person every two weeks. It happens so often that suicides rarely make the news in the Bay Area anymore.

An article by writer Ted Friend that appeared in the *New Yorker*[18] in 2003 includes an interview with Jerome Motto, a retired suicide expert from the Bay Area. Motto had a patient who committed suicide by jumping from the bridge in 1963, but he recalled another story from the 1970s that affected him profoundly.

Motto had accompanied the assistant medical director to the apartment of a man in his thirties who'd jumped from the bridge. According to Motto, the victim had written a note and left it in his apartment. The note said that he was going to walk to the bridge, and "'if one person smiles at me on the way, I will not jump.'"

Sadly, no one did.

Small Gestures, Huge Impact

Extending a Helping Hand is an aspect of leadership that, as we've discussed before, doesn't have to be herculean. As Motto's heart-wrenching anecdote suggests, it can even be something as simple as a smile. Indeed, any passers-by who would have taken the minuscule effort to smile at that unfortunate man as he made his way to the bridge that fateful day would have been unspoken leaders, perhaps even heroes, in their own right.

While the circumstances weren't nearly as dire, I remember one such gesture that has impacted my life ever since. One especially memorable figure who Extended a Helping Hand to me was John C. Maxwell. Yes, *the* John C. Maxwell: speaker extraordinaire, prolific best-selling author, and one of the most influential leadership gurus of our country.

Extending a Helping Hand doesn't have to be herculean.

I wrote Maxwell a letter a few years ago to ask for his forgiveness. You see, I had unknowingly borrowed some of his material and was using it in presentations across the country. In my letter, I introduced myself and gave some background on my career. The heart of my letter, however, explained that I had been giving a popular presentation around the country for years that touched on some of the same principles Maxwell had written about in one of his books, which I recently had come across.

I also apologized for what could be perceived as my stealing of his ideas (which, quite honestly, I hadn't) and asked what, if anything, he would like me to do with respect to continuing to give the presentation in question. In my heart of hearts, though I knew I hadn't intentionally done anything wrong, I came to realize that after discovering this potential issue, I had to make Maxwell aware of it. If the shoe was on the other foot, I reasoned, I would want someone else to do the same.

Understandably, I was on pins and needles as I awaited his response. And I had no idea how it would come: Would he write me back? Would he personally call me, irate and screaming and demanding money for what he might consider ripping off his ideas? Would his attorney ring me up, threatening me with all sorts of legal punishment? Would a sheriff drop off cease and desist papers?

On Christmas Eve, I had my answer, in the form of a handwritten note from John C. Maxwell himself, on his personal stationery, that arrived in the mail. It read:

Dave,

All is forgiven! You owe me nothing.

Continue to use the lecture to help others. The heart of your letter was evident and I applaud your desire to do right. Most of my material is a result of other people's thoughts. We are on the same team although we have never met. Adding value to others is a high calling!

John

There it was, in Maxwell's last sentence to me – the principle behind Extending a Helping Hand: Adding value to others is a high calling!

Leaders add value to the world around them. Whether you're leading a company, family, team, or classroom, Extending a Helping Hand is about positively impacting someone else's life, helping them in some way, by offering support, encouragement, knowledge, insight, or, in this situation, forgiveness.

Adding value to others is a high calling.

The Shaky Beginning Of Green Eggs And Ham

Consider the story of Theodor Seuss Geisel. You probably know him better by his pen name: Dr. Seuss. When Geisel wrote his first children's book, *And to Think That I Saw It on Mulberry Street,* it was rejected by 27 publishers.

However, a friend finally did Geisel a favor and published his work in 1937, which marked the start of one of the most successful careers in children's books. By the time Geisel died in 1991, his books had sold more than 200 million copies in 15 languages. Since then, his books have sold nearly a billion copies.

Can you imagine growing up without reading *The Cat in the Hat* or *Green Eggs and Ham?* Neither can I. But if it hadn't been for a friend Extending a Helping Hand to Geisel, the world would never have been blessed with the beautiful, inspirational quirkiness of Dr. Seuss.

In *Chicken Soup for the Unsinkable Soul,* actress Carol Burnett writes in her essay, "The Secret Behind My Success," of an anonymous donor who, after seeing her in an impromptu musical performance at a going-away party for one of her professors, offered to loan the aspiring actress $1,000 so she could move to

New York City to pursue a career in the entertainment industry.[19] There were only three stipulations of the loan: It was to be repaid in five years without interest, Burnett must never reveal the identity of her donor, and she must eventually pass along the kindness to help someone else.

Burnett finally accepted his offer – using some of the money to first go to the dentist and have two teeth extracted and filled, since she'd never been able to afford a dentist before – and made her way to the Big Apple. Like so many of her industry peers, she struggled for several years, her donated funds slowly dwindling, before she hit her big break. She collaborated along with several fellow struggling actors to put on their own show, which was a huge success.

Can you imagine growing up without The Cat in the Hat or Green Eggs and Ham?

That was just the ticket Burnett needed, and with several other theater companies and directors that had come calling, she was on her way. As her star continued to rise, she continued to keep her benefactor updated on her progress, but heard very little back from him. Five years to the day that she accepted his loan, she repaid it, and still counts his generosity – as well as what she learned about Extending a Helping Hand in the process – as a pivotal milestone in her remarkable career.

Givers Are Getters

It's been said that there are two kinds of people in the world: givers and takers. I actually think that both roles live inside each of us all the time and, depending on the situation or circumstance, one of them takes over.

But that doesn't mean we don't have a say in which is the stronger of the two. We *can* decide which one wins. So why not choose to be a giver instead of a getter?

Take a look at the people who are the givers. They're the ones who almost always seem to be filled up, happy, content.

Here's a practical way to put my secret to the test: the next time you get down about the circumstances in your life, give. Give of your time, your talent, or your treasure – just find a way to give. Find someone who is worse off than you and Extend a Helping Hand.

Your problems suddenly shrink when you give to others.

An amazing transformation will take place in your heart and mind: Your problems suddenly shrink when you give to others. You do not want to "trade" your pile of issues for theirs. In giving, you get: a better perspective, a better attitude, a better outlook.

I first discovered this truth while Extending a Helping Hand to a friend I was visiting in the hospital. I would love to tell you I was there because that's just the kind of guy I am: one who visits others in the hospital, but that would be a lie. Truth be told, I had been having quite a pity party for myself. I had just lost my largest customer to a competitor, my retirement investments had taken a major hit in the market, I was worried about having to let some employees go in a bad economy, my car had logged 200,000 miles and was making funny noises, my son was developing a real attitude *(and growing a Mohawk)* – you get the idea.

While griping about all of this at a family gathering, my ever-wise mother-in-law looked me square in the eye and said, "David, sounds like you need to get your eyes off yourself."

"What do you mean?" I asked.

"Whenever I feel down, I just go and find somebody who is worse off than me, and I help them in some way," she said. "You know what happens? My problems seem to shrink and I become very grateful for my blessings."

Her words became the motivation to go to the hospital to visit a friend who was recovering from an illness. While I was there, a nurse came into the room and asked me to step out for a few minutes so she could take care of some tasks. I didn't even want to know what that might entail – bedpans, bandages, and blood are all things I will gladly avoid.

So I began to roam the halls of the hospital. I wandered past the over-priced gift shop and meandered by the cafeteria. Eventually, I stumbled upon the interfaith chapel.

I pushed open the door, adorned with stained glass, and peeked inside. It was empty, so I stepped in. There was soft music playing, several rows of chairs, an altar with a kneeling pad, and a cross on the front wall with a table below it. On the table was a basket full of little cards upon which people had written their prayers.

Like a moth to light, I was drawn to the cards in the basket. I felt a little guilty as I picked one up, but I began to read it anyway: *"If there is any way you can heal my baby, please, I beg you, do it."*

I picked up another: *"Please take this away from my wife and give it to me."*

Card after card I read, my heart aching for people I would never know. Tears began to stream down my face as I continued to read. And then I came across a card I will never forget. Scrawled with a blue crayon were these words:

And then I came across a card I will never forget.

"Dear God, Please let Mommy live until Christmas. Love, Jenny"

My mother-in-law was right. Suddenly, I didn't have any problems. I thought I had gone to the hospital to "help" someone else who was worse off than me, you know, to "give" of myself. And while my friend was touched that I had come to wish him well, I was the one who came away from the visit full.

Mythological Makeover

While I was never a big fan of English class in high school, I still remember how much I enjoyed Greek mythology *(though I'd never have admitted it at the time)*. I ate up those fascinating stories of the gods, mortals, mythical creatures like Cyclops and Medusa, and the depths of the Underworld.

One story revolved around a lonely King named Pygmalion. Living on the Island of Cypress, he longed for someone to love and to love him in return. He ached for companionship.

So Pygmalion, who also had a knack for sculpture, set out to create a sculpture of a woman. Not just any woman, but *the* woman. Drawing from all the loneliness, heartache and emptiness in his soul, Pygmalion created a statue of breathtaking, magnificent beauty. He spent countless hours with her and showered her with compliments. He fell deeply in love with his creation and desired nothing else than to spend the rest of his life with her, but as a real woman.

As people learn of the expectations others have of them, they begin to be pulled in the direction of those expectations.

Driven almost mad with love for his sculpture, Pygmalion prayed to Aphrodite, the Greek goddess of love, and pleaded with her to bring his beautiful statue to life. Aphrodite was moved by Pygmalion's plea and, because he was a good and upright man, she came to earth and performed a big fat Greek makeover, transforming the chiseled stone into a flesh and blood woman. Pygmalion and his sculpture-turned-flesh-and-blood-woman were married and, as in all great love stories, lived happily ever after.

I share this myth because it forms the foundation for a modern-day concept. Perhaps you may have even heard the term but are not completely sure you know what it means: the Pygmalion Effect. Sociologists and behavioral researchers refer to the Pygmalion Effect as the ability to have transformative impact in the lives of others. Here's how it works: As people learn of the expectations others have of them, they begin to be pulled in the direction of those expectations, whether they're good or bad.

For example, as Pygmalion "interacted" with his sculpture, he did so in such a way as to communicate how amazing and warm and gracious she was, and ultimately she became that (with a little help from Aphrodite).

Mythology To Reality

Similar to the concept of the self-fulfilling prophecy, we tend to communicate our expectations of others in how we act, react, respond, and interact with them. If our thoughts and feelings toward others are negative, low, or discouraging, we tend to communicate those expectations through our words, body language, and tone of voice. And sure enough, when that happens, we tend to get exactly what we expected to get out of that person.

Conversely, if our thoughts, feelings, and expectations toward others are supportive and encouraging, we similarly communicate those positive things, and in the end, also tend to get what we expected out of those people. In this case, though, they're good things.

Harvard University researcher Robert Rosenthal illustrated this concept in dramatic fashion through a study with

Lenore Jacobson, an elementary school principal in San Francisco.[20] The pair set out to see if the expectations teachers have about their students' abilities could unwittingly influence their academic achievement, positively or negatively.

Having spent most of their adult lives in education, these two were concerned that teachers' expectations of minority and less privileged children were contributing to their high rates of academic failure. They saw firsthand that, when teachers expected students to fail, the students sure enough tended to fail.

When teachers expected students to fail, the students tended to fail.

But could a different expectation or influence have a positive impact? When teachers expected students to do well, would they tend to do well?

They set out to see with their revolutionary experiment. At the beginning of the school year, all the students in the school were "tested" to identify those who showed the highest level of academic potential, regardless of their previous academic results. The teachers were told that the test was called "The Harvard Test of Inflected Acquisition," and not only was this measurement capable of determining IQs, but it could also identify those students who would make rapid, above-average intellectual progress in the coming year. As teachers received their class lists for the year, they were also informed which of their students showed great potential, according to the test.

But the test was just a fake. In reality, Rosenthal and Jacobson randomly picked 20 percent of the students and then told their teachers that these kids showed "unusual potential for intellectual growth."[21]

At the end of the year, all the students were again tested. Those who had been labeled as "intelligent" children showed significantly greater increases than the other children who were not singled out as high-potential students, *and* they were identified by their teachers as better behaved, more intellectually curious, happier, and friendlier, with greater chances for future success. In other words, changes in the teachers' expectations regarding the intellectual performance of these allegedly "gifted" children had led to an *actual* change in the intellectual performance of these randomly selected children.

The teachers had subtly and unconsciously encouraged the performance they expected to see. Not only did they spend more time with these students, but also they were more enthusiastic about teaching them and unintentionally showed more warmth to them than to the other students. As a result, the random students felt more capable and intelligent. And they performed accordingly.

You see, these teachers taught the randomly selected children as if they really *were* something special. Virtually every aspect of their behavior communicated their belief in these kids. The Pygmalion Effect has real implications. As we communicate our expectations of others, we influence their expectations of themselves.

As leaders, one of our foremost responsibilities is to help those around us, in our spheres of influence, both discover and develop *their* potential. In fact, one very effective, but somewhat underused, leadership strategy is this: Don't try to get people to think more highly of *you;* try to get them to think more highly of *themselves.* Stated differently, as leaders we must be able to see the potential in others even before they can see it in themselves and learn to interact with them as though they are that more evolved version of themselves – because, deep down, most people evaluate their success by what others think.

> *Don't try to get people to think more highly of you; try to get them to think more highly of themselves.*

J. Sterling Livingston, a professor at Harvard Business School subsequently wrote an article called "Pygmalion in Management," which was followed up with a number of studies and experiments. The article and the studies illustrated that, just as with teachers and students, "A manager's expectations are key to a subordinate's performance and development."[22]

Leaders who believe in the potential of their team members and colleagues bring out the best in them by helping them believe in themselves, constantly challenging them to grow and supporting them along the way.

In other words, great leaders understand the influence they wield in helping others to reach *their* potential. One of the best ways to Extend a Helping Hand is to release in others the belief that they can do it. That they have what it takes. It's all about building up, positive encouragement, and words of life. (It's a concept I explained in depth my first book, *Sticks & Stones Exposed: The Power of Our Words.)*

Be A Wrangler, Not A Strangler

One story that's been circulated all over the internet, especially on self-help blogs, is about an undergrad literary club from the University of Wisconsin. The club was made up of male students who had shown a real knack in writing. This group, which included aspiring essayists, poets, and novelists, began to meet regularly to give each feedback on each other's work.

At club meetings, one student would stand up in front of the others and read aloud one of his works, followed by input from his fellow club members. Sounds helpful, right? Not exactly. The students were horribly mean in delivering their input, which was usually negative. They gave scathing critiques, often line by line, to the presenting member. The environment was so relentless that the club started calling themselves "The Stranglers."

That doesn't sound like any club I'd want to be a part of as a hopeful literary type. Instead, I'd have wanted to join "The Wranglers," an all-female literary group (which means that, alas, my gender would have presented a slight obstacle to that end). Like the Stranglers, this group's members also had exceptional talent and interest in writing and literature, but the atmosphere at their gatherings couldn't have been more different than that of the Stranglers' sessions. Instead of tearing down fellow members when presenting their work, the Wranglers delivered kind, thoughtful, constructive feedback, not caustic, cutting criticism. Their modus operandi was to lift each other up, to support and encourage one another in order to improve their talents.

Great leaders understand the influence they wield in helping others to reach their potential.

About two decades later, a researcher who'd heard about these groups decided to see what had happened to the members of both groups in their respective career fields. Turns out that not one of the aspiring talents in the Stranglers had achieved a literary reputation of any kind. But the Wranglers had produced several successful, well-known writers, among them, Marjorie Kinnan Rawlings, author of *The Yearling.*

It doesn't take a genius to consider what may have been the pivotal factor in determining the overall success of the groups' members. After all, the makeup and format of both groups were similar. Both had talented, passionate students as their members. But the difference was – you guessed it – that the Stranglers tore each other down, while the Wranglers lifted each other up.

In other words, while both groups sought to Extend a Helping Hand by offering members constructive criticism of their work, it would seem that the Stranglers' hands were far more hurtful than helpful.

So, when it comes to Extending a Helping a Hand, exactly *how* we do that is critical. While everyone needs to be critiqued once in a while – and leaders are often the ones to handle that task – no one is capable of reaching their potential, or being a happy human being, for that matter, when they're constantly criticized. In addition, when criticism is necessary *(like those employee evaluations everyone loves to hate)* it's so important to deliver it in a positive, uplifting, encouraging manner, rather than a derogatory, scathing one. In other words, be a Wrangler, not a Strangler.

The Lemonade Stand Of Life

I cannot drive past a lemonade stand without stopping. It's impossible. My DNA will not allow it. If I see some kids sitting at their ratty card table with a sign, a pitcher, and a stack of Dixie cups from their bathroom, I am hooked.

It is so fun to jump out, buy a cup of lemonade, introduce myself, shake their hands, and tell them how exciting it is to meet some young entrepreneurs. I tell them about how important it is to have businesses that create jobs and help provide income to families. I tend to never have the correct change for a cup of lemonade, so I tell them to keep the change and to reinvest the profits. I visit with the kids for at least 10 minutes.

You never outgrow the desire to hear that someone thinks you have what it takes.

As I drive away and look in my rear view mirror, they are all six inches taller. Why? Because now they see themselves as entrepreneurs who have what it takes to be somebody. And guess what else I have discovered? You never outgrow the desire to hear that someone thinks you have what it takes, that you can make a difference. I have been speaking professionally for 25 years, and I still love and need to hear that someone else believes in me and what I do, and thinks I have the ability to positively influence my audiences.

So I leave you with this thought: Make life a lemonade stand. As often as you can, Extend a Helping Hand to those around you.

EXPLORE ON YOUR OWN

1. Think back to a time when someone Extended a Helping Hand to you. Describe the incident. How did it make you feel?

2. Can you think of someone with whom you regularly interact who is a giver? Describe them and how they make it a point to give.

3. Think of someone you personally know who is in worse shape than you, however you define that. How can you Extend a Helping Hand to this person?

4. Why does helping someone else seem to benefit us so much?

5. How could the Pygmalion Effect happen in your life as you interact with others?

6. Identify someone of whom you may have negative expectations (or at least less than stellar). How will you communicate a different, more positive belief or expectation of them?

7. Name some ways you can get people close to you to think more highly of themselves.

8. Most everyone knows both Stranglers and Wranglers. What can you do to ensure that you are a Wrangler?

CHAPTER 11

LEADERSHIP REDEFINED, EVERY DAY

A life is not important except in the impact
it has on other lives.

~ Jackie Robinson

In his wonderful book, *The Sports 100: The 100 Most Important People in American Sports History,* author Brad Herzog highlights whom he believes are the 100 most important people in American sports history. When he comes to Jackie Robinson, it is as if he stops for a moment, takes a breath, and thinks, "Now this one is the most special of all." Herzog then goes on to explain how Robinson, who broke the color barrier in baseball and became the first African-American to play in the major leagues, is the most influential person in American sports history:

> *First, there are those who changed the way the games were played. ... Then there are the men and women whose presence and performance forever altered the sporting scene in a fundamental manner. ... And, finally, there are the handful of sports figures whose influence transcended the playing fields and impacted American culture. ... [Jackie] Robinson, to a greater extent than anyone else, was all three types in one.*"[23]

An Unsung Hero In Baseball And History

While Robinson became a household name, one man in particular who helped him ascend to the heights he did remains relatively unknown. That's right: There's an unsung hero in Robinson's already spectacular story, a man who embodied the principles in this book and acted as a leader even though he did not have any such title, obligation, or responsibility.

He was the guy who played next to Robinson on the Dodger infield: Harold Reese, better known as Pee Wee Reese.

And his story is remarkable.

Much in the same way that a chess pawn can be overshadowed and underappreciated, the name Pee Wee Reese often doesn't come up in a conversation about the history of baseball – or the Civil Rights movement in our country, for that matter.

But that's what Pee Wee Reese did. He helped Robinson break the color barrier in baseball, and as a result, provide much-needed momentum to the growing Civil Rights movement.

Now, Reese was not what one would have called a blue-chip prospect. In fact, he did not even play baseball in high school until his senior year because he was just too small (he earned his nickname as a champion marble shooter, interestingly enough). And even then, he only played in six games as a second baseman. Fortunately though, he played on his church's team, helping them reach the championship game.

The local minor league team, the Louisville Colonels, graciously offered their field for the championship game. During that game, the owner of the Colonels saw Reese play, and after the game he offered him a minor league contract for a $200 bonus.

Two years later, Reese had worked his way up to the big leagues and was the starting shortstop for the Brooklyn Dodgers. In his first major league season, he injured his foot and missed half the season. Reese's second year was a disaster. His batting average was dismal, and he led the majors with 47 errors *(definitely not what you would call leader-like stats)*. His breakout year was 1942, when everything seemed to come together and he made the National League All-Star team.

The next year, however, World War II interrupted Reese's baseball career, and he spent three years serving in the U.S. Navy in the Pacific theater. Aboard a ship bound for home from Guam, Reese heard some big news: His Dodgers had signed Robinson. As the news spread on the ship of Robinson's signing, the racial slurs started to flow.

Not only had the Dodgers signed an African-American, which was unheard of, but also troubling for Reese was the fact that he would be battling Robinson for the same starting position.

If we look closely at Reese's actions, we can see how the concepts of Leadership Redefined began to take effect. Even though he didn't hold any official leadership title, such as team captain, Reese began to use the strategies outlined in this book to positively impact the world around him.

There's an unsung hero in Robinson's already spectacular story.

Upon hearing the news about Robinson's acquisition with the Dodgers, Reese's first reaction was to **Exhibit an Attitude of Optimistic Confidence.** In an interview, Reese recalled thinking, "I had confidence in my abilities, and I thought, well, if he can beat me out, more power to him."[24]

Shortly after arriving back in the States, Reese would come face-to-face with Robinson as they both reported to Spring

Training. If there was racial tension on the ship coming home from Guam, it didn't even compare to the levels in the Dodgers locker room as players waited for Robinson to arrive.

In preparation, Reese **Explored All Possible Avenues** as he considered how he, *personally*, should act, react, and respond toward his new teammate, regardless of how others behaved. And with his decision made, Reese was the first teammate to walk across the field and, literally, **Extend a Helping Hand** to Robinson in the form of a handshake. In various reports, Reese said it was the first time he'd ever shaken the hand of a black man, having grown up during segregation.

Expecting Opposition, Reese prepared himself for the worst. And sure enough, it quickly reared its ugly head in the form of a petition drawn up by some of his teammates (mostly Southern Dodger players like himself), stating that they would not take the field with a black man. Reese's teammates thought that he, especially being a fellow Southerner, would join them in refusing to play. Reese, however, **Exceeded the Normal Expectations** that his teammates had of him and **Excluded their Negative Thinking** from his perspective.

Because he had already **Extracted a Goal** (playing Major League baseball and providing for his family), Reese **Expressed his Vision to Others,** and refused to sign the petition. He **Exchanged Non-Essentials** by refusing to get distracted by focusing on the wrong thing: the color of a teammate's skin. He said, "I just wanted to play baseball. I'd just come back from serving in the South Pacific in the Navy during the Second World War and I had a wife and daughter to support. I needed the money. I just wanted to get on with it."[25]

Reese refused to sign the petition, which then lost its momentum. Many believe that Reese's refusal to sign the petition was a pivotal moment that led to Robinson's eventual acceptance by his teammates in the Dodger clubhouse.

Jackie Robinson ended up making the Dodgers starting line-up, but not at shortstop, where Reese played. He began at first base and then was switched to second base. As the team headed out to begin the season, Reese again **Expected Opposition.**

Now, however, the opposition would be found in the fans and the opposing players. The bitter hatred and venom directed at Robinson was some of the most vicious ever known in sports. As Reese **Examined Everything,** he saw how Robinson's life was in real danger, from pitchers intentionally throwing at Robinson's head; to opposing base runners sharpening their metal spikes and trying to gouge him as they slid into second; to death threats against Robinson. But Reese once again **Excluded the Negativity** and **Explored all Possible Avenues** in deciding how to react, and, in what many believe to be the critical moment in Robinson's career, **Exhibited an Attitude of Optimistic Confidence** toward Robinson, as well as in his teammate's ability to rise above such horrible treatment from others.

The bitter hatred and venom directed at Robinson was some of the most vicious ever known in sports.

But the strongest testament of Reese's leadership came at Crosley Field in Cincinnati, when Robinson made an appearance in front of an unfamiliar crowd for the first time. During pre-game warm-ups, Cincinnati fans and players verbally attacked and heckled Robinson. Refusing to ignore, under such hostility, Reese walked across the infield, put his arm around Robinson's shoulder, and just stared down the jeering fans and players as if to say, "This is my guy, and I've got his back." Slowly the fans quieted down.

That very moment Robinson would later describe as one he would "never forget. It may have saved my career."

Though the Dodgers lost that game in Cincinnati, over the next decade, Reese and Robinson consistently **Exercised Effort** to become one of the deadliest double play combinations in baseball. Eventually, they both earned entry into the Hall of Fame.

Throughout this incredible journey, Reese had no official title. He was not in charge of player development. He was just one part of a team that played 43 men that year. A pawn, you might say. But just three short years later, during which he demonstrated the Leadership Redefined strategies that have been identified in this book, "unofficial captain" Pee Wee Reese was officially named the Captain of the Brooklyn Dodgers.

In addition, Reese's influence reached far beyond baseball. The pivotal moment when he put his arm around Robinson is now depicted in a bronze sculpture by sculptor William Behrends, with Reese's arm draped over his teammate's shoulder. The sculpture was unveiled on November 1, 2005, at KeySpan Park in Brooklyn. It still stands as a testament to how such a simple action could make such a powerful statement about the atrocities of bigotry and racial discrimination.[26]

Leadership Redefined Every Day

I've illustrated how Pee Wee Reese was a living embodiment over the course of several years of the principles in this book. But part of the universal appeal and practicality of Leadership Redefined is that you can apply it to your daily life – and integrate it into your thoughts, behavior, and interactions.

When I tackled this chapter (and, quite honestly, every single one in this book!), I had to **Extract a Goal** to get a rough draft down. Writing doesn't come naturally to me, so it takes considerable effort and focus to do this. And in order to make that happen, I had to both **Expect Opposition** and **Exchange Non-Essentials** in the form of my own internal doubts and outside interruptions. In other words, I had to let the more mundane aspects of my job go for a few hours. So I told my colleagues I was going off the grid for most of the day, turned off my cell phone, and sequestered myself in a quiet room with my laptop so that I could concentrate on the most important task at hand: finishing this chapter, which was part of the bigger goal to write this book.

As is the case with many full-time writers, I also battled serious self-criticism throughout the project. I had to **Exclude Negative Thinking** and ignore the little voices in my head that told me I couldn't do it and wouldn't be able to write anything of worth. Instead, I **Expressed My Vision to Others** and **Exposed Myself to Winners** – especially my wife, Tina, to whom I'd read a paragraph (or 20) for constructive criticism. I also replaced my own negative thinking by **Exhibiting an Attitude of Optimistic Confidence,** reminding myself that I'd written a book before and could do it again.

Everyone has the ability to start putting the principles of Leadership Redefined to work in their lives immediately.

I **Explored All Possible Avenues** and **Examined Everything** throughout the process, too. I consulted various resources and experts to validate my ideas. I **Exceeded Normal Expectations** as I considered different ways to express an idea or illustrate a concept. I went through many different anecdotes to find the best ones that supported the principles.

Of course, it was hard work. But I **Exercised Effort,** the final result of which is in your hand right now. And lastly, I hope to **Extend a Helping Hand** to positively impact your life with the principles I have shared in this book.

Small Changes, Big Results

While there are 12 principles that together make up Leadership Redefined, they go hand-in-hand. They complement and support each other. So when you make an effort to concentrate on one or two, it becomes that much easier to eventually work all of them into your daily life: at work, at home, at school, with family, with friends, with just about any interaction you have, personally, professionally, casually, and spiritually.

Of course, some of them will probably come easier for you than others. For example, Exchanging Non-Essentials will always be a concerted effort for me, because I'm easily distracted by urgent, but not necessarily important, issues, via the barrage of technology that inundates us these days. However, when I look at the importance of Exchanging Non-Essentials with respect to Extracting a Goal, for example, I realize how critical it is to focus on the important things – and I'm more inclined to get my priorities in order, as with this project.

There can never be too many people doing the right thing.

And therein lies what I believe is the most important message in this book: Everyone has the ability to start putting the principles of Leadership Redefined to work in their lives immediately. Remember Marvin, the rental car shuttle driver, Miss Hannah, the cafeteria lady, and Fanny Crosby, the blind hymn writer? They were incredible leaders in their own right. By the way they treated other people, brought incredible enthusiasm to their jobs, and radiated optimism and a positive attitude, they truly influenced the world around them.

Indeed, when we look a little closer, we can see that leaders are all around us. But the world desperately needs more. There can never be too many people doing the right thing. By finishing this book and understanding that there is plenty more to being a leader than titles or authority, you're well on your way to realizing YOU ARE A LEADER.

One of the world's greatest leaders, Nelson Mandela, once said that we were born to manifest the glory that is within us. So I urge you to implement these 12 strategies into your life to help you achieve that glory, by influencing the world around you in a positive, uplifting way. Lead well!

EXPLORE ON YOUR OWN

1. On the chessboard of life, why is it easy to overlook a pawn? How does this apply to you?

2. Of the 12 Leadership Redefined strategies that Pee Wee Reese demonstrated, which do you think would have been the most difficult for you? Why?

3. When Reese went against most of his Southern teammates, he was actually fighting for Robinson. Is there someone in your life now who seems to have everyone unfairly and undeservedly pitted against them? How can you fight for that person?

4. Is there an area in your life right now that you need to Expect Opposition in? How will this strategy help you in the accomplishment of your goal?

5. How can Expressing Your Vision to Others help get others on your side, moving toward the same outcome or shared goal?

6. What are some non-essentials you need to purge from your life? When and how will you do that?

7. Name an area in your life where you have allowed some negative attitudes to sneak in. What do you need to do to eliminate those thoughts and attitudes? What should you focus on instead?

8. Identify three or four strategies in this book that you are going to put some effort into first. Why? How? When?

Turn the page to read the first chapter of Dave and Logan's best seller *Sticks & Stones Exposed.*

Available now at
webermotivation.com

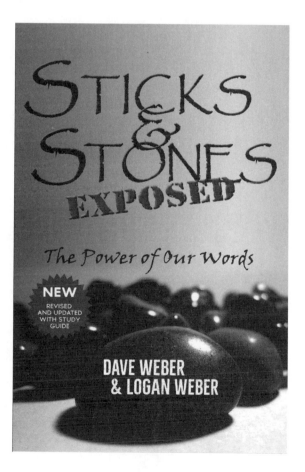

Chapter 1

Sticks and Stones

An injury is much sooner forgotten than an insult.
– Lord Chesterfield

The brisk New England wind whistled loudly through the trees that cold afternoon as seven-year-old Davey raced home from school, but the only thing he could hear was the chilling echo of his classmates' taunts. *"SHRIMPUS! SHRIMPUS!"* the other boys and girls shrieked over and over just moments ago, chanting in a frenzied mob at the bus stop. The word crushed Davey's heart like a sledgehammer on limestone. He ran from the bus stop as fast as he could, the wind whipping at his face, his tears nearly frozen as they streamed from his eyes, his spirit as dark and gray as the winter sky.

He finally arrived home, flinging open the door and heading toward the comfort and solitude of his bedroom. But his tear-streaked cheeks gave away his troubles as he tried to slip past his father, who gathered him up and asked what was wrong. Davey began sobbing again as he relived the horrible episode: the taunts, the teasing, the scathing nickname he knew he'd never forget. "Son," his father said, bending down to his level and pulling him close, "you need to remember that sticks and stones may break your bones, but words will never hurt you."

"But, Daddy," Davey sniffled, looking up at his father with teary blue eyes. "They *did* hurt me. They hurt me in my heart."

More than thirty winters have come and gone since I (Dave) sought comfort in the arms and words of my father that day. While his hug soothed me, his words didn't. Even as a seven-year-old boy, I knew they weren't true – after all, that was real pain I felt, even though it didn't leave a visible bruise or scar.

As an adult, I traded New England nor-easters for milder temperatures in the suburbs of Atlanta, with two school-aged children of my own. It was not long before I found myself biting back that same childhood rhyme as my kids encountered the sticks and stones of playground taunts and bus stop bullies. But, my own children could not outrun the hurtful words the way I could all those years ago. No, with AIM messaging, and then much later texting and social media, sticks and stones were sailing into my house, and I felt like I had no idea how to defend my family from the onslaught and the childhood rhyme simply was not working.

> *"Sticks and stones may break your bones,*
> *But words will never hurt you."*

Many of us reference this little phrase when we're trying to console someone we care about after they've been "hurt in their heart." "Sticks and stones" is a mantra handed down from generation to generation, helping children deal with the sting of the big, cruel world and the nasty people they'll inevitably encounter in it. Our hearts are in the right place in trying to help kids rationalize their hurt feelings with that little rhyme, but the logic isn't. Words *do* hurt – in fact, according to some research, emotional pain is processed in the same part of the brain as physical pain.

And that emotional pain can result in something much worse than a broken bone. Broken bones mend themselves, sometimes growing stronger than they were before, but harmful words and behaviors can result in lifelong injury. They break our hearts, scratch our spirits, and dent our self-esteem, all of which

> Broken bones mend themselves but harmful words and behaviors can result in lifelong injury.

is damage that may never fully heal. That damage can also manifest itself in detrimental physical ways.

A study done in 1999 by W. Penn Handwerker, a professor of anthropology at the University of Connecticut, Storrs, linked depression, suicide, stress, heart disease, and even the aggression witnessed in the Littleton, Colorado, public school shootings with a lifetime of harboring hurtful words from others. Handwerker's research looked at the effects of childhood violence – not just physical violence like hitting or slapping – but belittling and demeaning behavior, treating someone as inferior, and attempting to make people feel bad about themselves. Handwerker's research is just one of dozens of studies that have illustrated the incredible impact of negative words.

Clearly, words matter. They're powerful. And what matters most is *how* we use them. Do we use them like sticks and stones, to tear down, to destruct, and destroy? Or, do we use them to build up, encourage, and affirm?

A Rising Epidemic

The power of words is not a new or revolutionary concept. English novelist Edward George Bulwer Lytton, who died in

1873, once wrote, "The pen is mightier than the sword." Go thousands of years further back and you find the wisdom of King Solomon, "Death and life are in the power of the tongue . . ." In a more modern-day light, we were taught as youngsters the premise of the Golden Rule, perhaps the most mainstream and timeless ethical standard for behavior. It states "Do unto others as you would have them do unto you" (No healthy, self-respecting individual who would consider name-calling or belittling, negative statements – all of which are forms of sticks and stones – as part of behavior he or she would like directed at them). There are also countless examples in pop culture that address the potential impact of words. In Taylor Swift's 2011 single, "Mean" she sings "You, with your words like knives and swords and weapons that you use against me."

What's so amazing about words is that they're so easily uttered, yet so difficult to forget.

What's so amazing about words is that they're so easily uttered, yet so difficult to forget once they've been tossed out there. While most of us can't even recall the details of our day-to-day life experiences – what we ate for dinner last Thursday, which clothes we wore on Monday, what we did last weekend – our minds act like virtual DVRs when it comes to the spoken word. They harbor a collection of all those ugly things people have said to us, effortlessly recording and playing back mean comments from years and years ago, even if the person who did the damage may not remember it a few days later. And, on the flip side, the positive, uplifting, supportive

Our minds act like virtual DVRs when it comes to the spoken word.

words stick in our minds, too. Every person reading this book has their own recollection of something especially positive a teacher, parent, or friend once said to them. We reflect on those comments, praise, and encouragements throughout our lives, whether we were five or fifty when we heard them.

Unfortunately, though, it seems the negative stuff is much more prevalent these days. Sticks and stones are being tossed all over the place. Just take a peek into any high school setting or on any social media platform, where trolling is considered much cooler than an honest compliment any day. An estimated 117 million Americans listen to or share gossip about other people at least once or twice a week, according to a poll commissioned by the non-profit organization WordsCanHeal.org. Flip on a television and take your pick of evidence: talk shows whose guests are verbally bashing each other in front of a national audience, reality shows with contestants who criticize teammates and cut down opponents on a regular basis. Road rage, a nonexistent term less than twenty years ago, has become an everyday word in our vocabularies, as stressed-out drivers hurl streams of threats, insults, and obscenities at one another during rush hour traffic.

The examples go on and on. Researchers estimate that hundreds of thousands of children are teased and taunted every day at school. Rudeness is on the rise nationwide, according to a two-year survey released in 2002 called "Aggravating Circumstances: A Status Report on Rudeness in America." Conducted by Public Agenda, a nonprofit research arm of The Pew Charitable Trusts, this extensive survey found a whopping 79 percent of Americans say a lack of respect and courtesy should be regarded as a serious national problem – and 60 percent say that things are getting worse. Recently, some behavioral experts have coined a term, relational aggression, or RA, that suggests a disturbing trend developing among youngsters. It describes a variety of behaviors engaged in by children that harm others by damaging, or threatening to damage, one's relationship with his or her peers. Found to be more common in girls than boys, RA can be spreading rumors, purposefully ignoring others, or telling others not to play with a certain individual.

There's so much nastiness out there that some entrepreneur has made a fast buck off a simple but true societal slogan splashed on T-shirts and bumper stickers everywhere: "Mean People Suck." And then there's the related nationwide epidemic of increasing violence, in our schools, on our streets, and sometimes even in our homes.

Not a pretty picture, is it? So why can't we just drop our sticks, let our stones fall to the ground, and *all just get along?*

The answer is – as you're about to discover – because just getting along involves a lot more than we realize.

Even Golden Rule Gurus Need Help

You might be thinking, *Well, I'm not one of those mean people they talk about on bumper stickers. I don't ever exhibit road rage. I don't post or retweet ugly comments about others. I'm not part of that national rudeness epidemic. I live my life by the Golden Rule and I always treat other people with respect and encouragement!*
Good for you! But consider this:

○ Have you ever found yourself the *target* of sticks and stones thrown out by others **who had no clue** about the damaging consequences of their words or actions?

○ Have you told a friend, a boss, a spouse: "I felt very hurt by what you said/did/conveyed through your behavior?"

○ Have you ever thought, "I didn't like how that person treated me?" or "His words really stung?" or "Is that post about me?"

If that's the case, isn't there at least a chance that you've done the same exact thing to someone else, without even realizing it either?

Even if you're not the kind of person who fires off troll tweets for Likes, insulting remarks, or degrading comments like rocks from a slingshot, at some point in your life your words, posts, texts, or behaviors have hurt those around you. After all, actions can mean omissions too: They can be the things you don't do, you forget to do, or you simply don't think are important. When was the last time you told your child that she has brought so much joy into your life? Or your husband that you appreciate all his hard work? Or your co-worker that she did a great job on her presentation?

Your non-verbal behavior is just as important. What kind of message might you be sending with your basic body language? Without saying a word, we can throw sticks and stones at those around us. With rolled eyes. With crossed arms. With sighs. Even with silence.

If any of the above sounds familiar, you'll definitely get something out of this book. And even if you've already told yourself that the above paragraphs don't exactly describe you – you're a boss who praises her employees regularly; a husband who tells his wife she looks beautiful every day; a parent who encourages his children constantly – our hope is that this book will help you, too, by allowing you to discover a more effective way of affirming others in your life.

Therein lies one of our primary objectives in writing this book: to be a catalyst for some positive changes in your life. Changed perspectives. Changed beliefs. Ultimately, changed relationships and lives.

Intentional Affirmation

Several years ago, talk show icon and national celebrity Oprah Winfrey aired an episode that remains one of her most memorable to date. It featured "random acts of kindness" – unprompted, benevolent gestures that included paying the toll of the following car at the toll booth or anonymously donating sums of money to charity. This particular show made quite an impact on both the people who were featured as well as Oprah's viewing audience, causing a domino-like effect of positive behavior. People who'd been granted the "random acts" often returned the favor immediately, paying the fare for the car behind them, donating money to a charitable cause, or performing similar simple, kind acts for others.

When we hear about the kind actions of our fellow humans like this, it often strikes some sort of a good-nature chord within our spirits, doesn't it? We're awash in the warm glow of the decency of human nature, and we often feel moved enough to do some good of our own.

Furthermore, don't we say that an underlying motivation for various forms of altruism – treating others with kindness, volunteering our time, even offering a simple smile to a stranger on the street – is the sense of happiness *we* feel in doing such things? In other words, it's not just that we're making someone else's world brighter; it's the sense of accomplishment, of satisfaction, that indescribable "feel-good" factor that really inspires our own philanthropic efforts.

The point in all of this: If affirming others is so positive for us and our lives – not to mention the lives of those whom we are affirming – we need to do it intentionally, with purpose, all the time. This is a *conscious decision* to support, encourage, and lift up others every day of our lives. These concepts go beyond just dishing out an offhanded compliment here or a random act of kindness there. It's deeper than that.

But it's not rocket science, either. And it's not some far-fetched, left-field hypotheses about human nature. Our ideas are fairly simple, supported by a combination of research, common-sense knowledge, trends in society, and even some ancient literature. Once we started exploring these concepts a little bit further, we found evidence of their power everywhere we looked. In interactions among colleagues at the office. At the dinner table. Online and even between strangers in the doctor's office.

One . . . Two . . . Three . . .

Before we go any further, we need to go over three points you need to keep in mind while reading. These will help you understand and apply the concepts we'll be discussing.

1). **You are a whole person.** You may often define yourself in terms of your occupation, background, marital status, or hobbies, but those are just separate aspects of your life. However, you're not *just* an employee, *just* a parent, or *just* a friend – who you are as a person relates to the unique combination of all those different roles. The principles we'll discuss apply across the board to these roles in your life. You can apply them at the conference table, at the dinner table, and everywhere in between. And we encourage you to use them as widely as you can – they're much too powerful and effective to confine to just one area.

2). You have a *desire* to learn. Let's face it: we're not naive enough to think that every one of you reading this book picked it up on your own – you might be reading it as suggested by your manager or spouse (in which case, please keep reading – you'll end up thanking them for it). Whatever the case – if you're here for fun, by force, or for personal interest – you're here because your goal is to learn something.

3). You're a changing person. In the words of 1920s advertising baron Bruce Barton, "When you're through changing, you're through." If you haven't heard that phrase before, you've certainly heard this one (or some version of it): "The only constant in life is change." If change is a given, then what we hope to influence is the direction of that change. Which way are you headed in your emotional and behavioral development as a person? Are you progressing or regressing? By sharing these principles, we hope to push you on a forward-moving track.

One last note before we dig in: All of the stories and anecdotes in this book are based on actual experiences and events. Sometimes they are narrated in the first person with a parenthetical explanation to let you know who's talking, Dave or Logan. In other instances, a story is told in third-person for clarity. Additionally, some names have been omitted or changed.

LET'S TALK ABOUT IT

1. "Sticks and stones may break your bones but words will never hurt you" is a saying that has been shared for decades. What are some of the dangers of this rhyme?

2. Describe a recent interaction when you saw just how untrue the sticks and stones rhyme is.

3. Spoken words are not the only way we throw sticks and stones. Name other ways we do this. How can these other ways be even more hurtful and damaging than spoken words?

4. In your opinion, what are some of the factors that have led to this increase in society's throwing of "sticks and stones?"

5. Can you think of a time when you unintentionally hurt someone else with your words, actions, social media posts or attitudes? Describe it.

6. What are some factors that you believe have contributed to you personally throwing sticks and stones? (i.e. feeling tired, hungry, overwhelmed, taken for granted.)

7. Do you believe that "the conscious decision to support, encourage, and lift up others," can actually create quantifiable change? If so, how?

8. Name some of the benefits of encouraging others – at home, at work, at the grocery store, online.

9. Identify three people that you want to intentionally affirm starting tomorrow. What do you hope will be the result?

10. Why do you think the authors want you to read this book as a "whole person"?

11. Spend a moment reflecting on how your attitudes and perspectives have changed in the past few years. Do you think you have become a more positive or negative person? Why do you think that is?

12. What was your main takeaway from this chapter?

To order Dave and Logan's best seller *Sticks & Stones Exposed: The Power of Our Words*, go to:

webermotivation.com

END NOTES

[1] Ammeson, Jane. *World Traveler Magazine.* May 2001. Pgs. 40-43.

[2] Evans, Mike. *The Light.* Time Worthy Press, Phoenix, 2011. Anecdote listed on book's website, www.thelightbymikeevans.com.

[3] Mackay, Harvey. "Never underestimate the power of observation." *Orange County Register,* Feb. 12, 2007. Mackay Envelope Corp., 2100 Elm St., Minneapolis, MN, 55414.

[4] 1 Thessalonians: 5:21, *New American Standard Bible: The Open Bible Edition.* Thomas Nelson Publishers: Nashville, Tenn., 1979. © The Lockman Foundation, La Habra, California.

[5] Seidman, Dan. *The Death of 20th Century Selling.* Sales Autopsy Press, 2002. Pg. 88.

[6] 1 Samuel 17:30. *The Amplified Bible.* Zondervan Bible Publishers, Grand Rapids, Michigan: 1987.

[7] *People* magazine, April 12, 1982, Vol. 17, No. 14.

[8] Maruta T., Colligan RC, Malinchoc M., Offord KP. "Optimists vs Pessimists: Survival Rate Among Medical Patients Over a 30-Year Period." *Mayo Clin Proc.* 2000; 75:140-143.

[9] Levy, Becca R., and Slade, Martin D., Yale University; Kunkel, Suzanne R., Miami University, and Kasl, Stanislav V., Yale University. "Longevity Increased by Positive Self-Perceptions of Aging," *Journal of Personality and Social Psychology.* 2002, Vol. 83, No. 2, 261–270.

[10] Giltay, Erik J. M.D., Ph.D; Geleijnse, Johanna M., Ph.D; et al; "Cardiovascular Mortality in a Prospective Cohort of Elderly Dutch Men and Women." *Archives of General Psychiatry,* 2004; 61:1126-1135.

[11] Saavedra, Richard, University of Michigan, et al. "The Contagious Leader: Impact of the Leader's Mood on the Mood of Group Members, Group Affective Tone, and Group Processes." *Journal of Applied Psychology.* 2005, Vol. 90, No. 2. Pgs. 295–305.

12 Krakovsky, Marina. "When Feelings Come to Work." http://marinakrakovsky.com/business/wham_200604. html

http://intentionalworkplace.com/2011/02/03/leader-ship-and-emotional-contagion/

13 Seidman, Dan. *The Death of 20th Century Selling.* Pgs. 168-169.

14 Biro, Brian D. Beyond Success: *The 15 Secrets to Effective Leadership and Life Based on Legendary Coach John Wooden's Pyramid of Success.* The Berkeley Publishing Group: New York, 1997. Pg. 141.

15 Background information for this anecdote came from the following sources: http://www.inspiring-quotes-and-stories.com/disaster, and *The New York Times,* Dec. 10, 1914. Pgs. 1, 3.

16 Canfield, Jack; Hansen, Mark Victor; McNamara, Heather. *Chicken Soup for the Unsinkable Soul: 101 Inspirational Stories of Overcoming Life's Challenges.* Health Communications, Inc.: Deerfield Beach, Fla., 1999. Pgs. 257-259.

17 Hurlock, Elizabeth B. "An Evaluation of Certain Incentives used in School Work," *Journal of Educational Psychology,* 1925. Volume XVI, Number 3. Pgs. 145-159.

[18] Friend, Tad. "Jumpers: The fatal grandeur of the Golden Gate Bridge," *The New Yorker.* Oct. 13, 2003.

[19] Canfield, Jack; Hansen, Mark Victor; McNamara, Heather. *Chicken Soup for the Unsinkable Soul: 101 Inspirational Stories of Overcoming Life's Challenges.* Health Communications, Inc.: Deerfield Beach, Fla., 1999. Pgs. 80-84.

[20] Rosenthal, R. & Jacobson, L. *Pygmalion in the Classroom: Teacher Expectation and Students' Intellectual Development.* New York: Holt, Rinehart & Winston, 1968.

[21] Schugurensky, Daniel. "History of Education: Selected Moments of the 21st Century (A work in progress)." Department of Adult Education, Community Development and Counseling Psychology, The Ontario Institute of Studies in Education of the University of Toronto.

[22] Livingston, Sterling J. "Pygmalion in Management." *Harvard Business Review.* Jan. 1, 2003.

[23] Herzog, Brad. *The Sports 100: The 100 Most Important People in American Sports History.* New York: MacMillan, 1995. Pg. 7.

[24] Berkow, Ira. *The New York Times* website, Sports of the Times, "Standing Beside Jackie Robinson, Reese Helped Change Baseball." March 31, 1997.

[25] Berkow, Ira. "Standing Beside Jackie Robinson, Reese Helped Change Baseball."

[26] In addition to the book sourced in the previous end note, information from the following sources was used for the anecdote involving Pee Wee Reese:

Eig, Jonathon, *Opening Day: The Story of Jackie Robinson's First Season.* New York: Simon & Schuster Paperback, 2007. Pg. 35.

www.peeweereese.com, The Official Site of Pee Wee Reese.

Author Dave Weber is President/CEO of Weber Associates, a training and speaking company based in Atlanta, Georgia. An internationally recognized speaker, Weber conducts training and motivational programs for thousands of people every year in education, government, medical/dental and corporations such as:

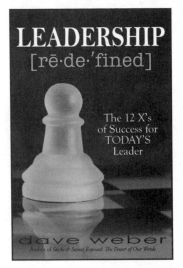

- The Weather Channel
- FedEx
- Chick-fil-A
- Cintas
- Bank of America
- Delta Airlines
- and many others

To contact Dave Weber or Weber Associates regarding additional copies of *Leadership Redefined: The 12 X's of Success for TODAY'S Leader* visit: **webermotivation.com**

If you are interested in speaking engagements, or to request additional information about Weber Associates, please visit: **webermotivation.com**

You can also call **1-800-800-8184** or **770-422-5654.**

975 Cobb Place Blvd., Suite 107
Kennesaw, GA 30144
1-800-800-8184
www.webermotivation.com